I0158331

Novel

Novel

LYNN BARRETT-LEE

LUME BOOKS

LUME BOOKS

First published in 2021 by Lume Books
30 Great Guildford Street,
Borough, SE1 0HS

ISBN 978-1-83901-383-6

Typeset using Atomik ePublisher from Easypress Technologies

www.lumebooks.co.uk

For all my former students,
Teaching you has taught me more than you know.

'I've written because it fulfilled me. Maybe it paid off the mortgage on the house and got the kids through college, but those things were on the side – I did it for the buzz. I did it for the pure joy of the thing. And if you can do it for joy, you can do it forever.'

Stephen King,
On Writing

Introduction

The passing on of stories is as old as mankind, and the urge to tell them, for many of us, runs deep. Those of us who find ourselves afflicted by the writing disease will know only too well that the true writer can't *not* write. Not for very long, anyway. As was so eloquently stated by the author Gracie Harmon, we are "just people who have a whole lot on the inside that they need to get to the outside, with pen and paper as their preferred method of transport".

Writers, in the main, write compulsively; we enjoy creating fiction out of the facts all around us, and even if we're not all scribbling furiously in cafes, then we're often to be found, miles away, staring into space, while engaged in doing likewise in our heads.

As stated so baldly underneath the title, this is a course for anyone who has a book currently in them that they'd prefer to see sitting in a bookshop. The naked ambition implied here is entirely intentional. Yes, we must write what we must write, as will be discussed at length later, but I have met and taught a lot of aspiring writers in my time and my not terribly scientific but still true conclusion is that they can broadly be classified into three types. These are the hobbyist, who has written much, over many years, and still gets a kick from it: these people tend to come to classes to hone craft, mix with other writers, feel energized and positive about what they do. Then there's the purist, who romanticises the muse and everything to do with it: these people tend to come to classes because they want to 'feel' like writers and they adore everything about the business of being one, bar that nagging voice (i.e. mine) that blathers on about treating it like something as vulgar and concrete as a 'job'. Then there's the third type, the type I see myself reflected back in (though I have also been and probably will be both those other types at different life-stages). They have come to classes because they want to be jobbing writers – and they want that pretty passionately. They want 'author' to be the word they use when asked for their 'occupation'. Making a living from writing, for such people, is the Holy Grail, the life's ambition, the be all and end all. For them, that space on a bookshop shelf (be it actual or virtual) matters very, very much.

Of the three broad kinds of writers there are many subtle sub-categories, too, about which we could analyse, even gently tease, at length. The embittered type 3, who, five novels in, has not yet had a sniff of an agent; the twitched type 2, who suspects their preferred writing method might not quite be working; the suddenly extra-enthused type 1, who has a grandchild at the reading stage and wants to redouble their efforts… There are others, too – and, let's be clear, a sense of humour about all this is vital – but most importantly, there's a sub-division common to all of them. Some write a little, some rather more, and some a *lot*.

While any writing is good, writing lots is even better. And if you want to make a living at it, writing lots is non-negotiable. If you want to become good at anything, it's important that you practice, so it's from this furiously writing group, in my experience (and almost without exception) that success, of a commercial kind, comes. Which is not the only kind of success, obviously, and neither should it be, for obvious reasons, but my assumption is that for most people reading this, that's the goal. In which case, you have come to the right place.

So, what will you find here? Well, for much of the time, what you'll find here will be questions. Questions every budding (and not so budding) writer has probably asked themselves at some point in their writing lives. What are the key components that every novel needs, and how can you use them to make your novel unputdownable? How can you ensure that your readers are enthralled? How should you use dialogue? How do you get a handle on chapters, hooks and cliffhangers? And once you've done all of that, how do you find the wherewithal to keep going? And once you've done *that*, how the heck do you find an agent?

Taking you step by step through the novel creation process and beyond, my aim is to guide you towards the answers that will work best for you. I don't claim that it's the most comprehensive guide to everything writing-related you'll ever want to know – because it's not; it's my ten week novel writing workshop recreated in a short, handy book; a distillation of things I've learned over many writing years. And if it's not something I've come across, had experience of, or learned from, then it's not going to be found here – how could it be? But as I say to my students, I'll always try to sleuth out an answer on your behalf, so why not email via my website? Happy to help.

I'm also making a couple of key assumptions at the outset. That you're not entering into the novel writing process cold. That you write. That you have written. That you've mastered most of the basics. That you already feel you have a bag of fiction-writing tricks, a facility with language, and are confident to make the leap so many writers aspire to – to think *bigger* now; to write a whole novel.

Of course, much of what you need you will need to find within you. No one can teach talent, imagination, resilience, doggedness, or drive. But if you have those, and are genuinely committed to writing that book you have in you, then there's much that *can* be taught. Welcome to the course.

Step 1 : Getting Started

The seven key ingredients

There are many ways to go about writing a novel. Indeed, 'Ways To Write A Novel' is a constant in the writing-related press, with pretty much every publication having its take on the subject, from 'My Writing Day', to 'How I Write Books', to 'I did it my way', and 'well, I *didn't*', and so on.

It reality, it's simpler than that. Broadly, you can choose between just two general camps: the 'start writing and see where it takes you' band of brothers or the 'plan to the nth degree before you pen a word' brigade. (It is from one of these philosophies that you will instinctively take your writing credo, even if, when it comes to it, you end up somewhere in the middle, letting the muse and your planning hold roughly equal sway.)

Clearly, if you are at the extreme end of the first group, you shouldn't be reading this book. I mean, I'm glad you are, obviously, because it means you're at least open to the possibility that reading around the subject might be helpful, and, let's be clear, I'm very happy that you bought it. However, writers who are committed to letting novels write themselves are generally so busy trying to unravel the resulting chaos that they have little time free to read how-to books.

But if, like me, you find the prospect of penning 80,000+ words without the least idea what they're going to be and quite where you're going to put them OR if you have been a long time subscriber to the first group and as a result have a number of third-of-the-way-through-and-then-gave-up-in-despair manuscripts to your name (as opposed to a bestseller), then there is hopefully much for you here. Which is because the purpose of this course is to deconstruct and analyse the novel-writing process and, though everyone will end up doing things slightly – or very – differently, to identify the key elements that are amenable to thought and planning, and which will, given a modicum of talent, imagination and continuing commitment, see you through to that 80,000th word…

This step, being our first, locates us at the beginning of the process, so we will address a number of things that need to be settled, at least provisionally, before we have anything to create a novel from.

Theme

You might have several ideas in mind, but which one has the strongest, most personally compelling feel to it? A theme, in this case, can be thought of as your novel's central preoccupation, so it probably needs to be something that you think – or have thought – a lot about, or, better still, had personal experience of i.e. bereavement and its consequences, jealousy, betrayal, a personal journey of some sort, marital relationships, sibling rivalry etc. No, it's not true that you should always try to write about what you know – that's ridiculous; you're not stupid – you can find stuff you don't know out. But, to some degree, you should perhaps lean towards writing about what you *feel*. Not with all your characters, obviously, because that would be unrealistic, but if your central character shares a powerful emotion with you, the author, that clarity of expression will greatly add to your writing.

Nailing your theme, early on, is a very useful thing to do. And not difficult: If someone asked 'what is your novel about?' (and they will) how would you answer them in one or two sentences? (Very useful for when you're published and guesting on Radio Sheffield…)

Setting

Where and when are you going to set the story in which you are going to explore your chosen theme? Will it be contemporary or historical or set in the future? Will it be a place and environment (social or career-based) that you know well, or will it require lots of research? There is no right or wrong here – no best choice or poor choice. Indeed, a strong urge to write in/about a certain place and time is usually a great predictor of passion for the project, which will support you whenever things get tough. What matters is that you are aware of the implications of your choice for the length and complexity of the task.

So, consider: Is the setting integral to the theme and/or plot? This is an important consideration, as it will impact on your progress at every turn, particularly if you choose a setting/environment that's unfamiliar to you, as noted above. Clearly, a book set in the Second World War will require research so that the details ring true. This might be a plus for you – if the process of information gathering appeals to you, go do it!

Conversely, there is little point in putting your characters in an exotic location just because it's somewhere you've been, want to visit, want to write about for reasons of 'glamour', or – a common one – think Richard and Judy/every book group in Britain (hell, the world) is going to like. Yes, a scenic 'destination' location has its own cachet, but don't stick your characters in, say, Rome, just to 'add a bit of colour'. Only do so because you need them to interact with their location in a meaningful way to explore your theme.

Viewpoint

Viewpoint (or POV) is straightforward. You can either write in first person ('**I** went to the shop') or third person ('**he/she/they** went to the shop'). There are variations – alternate chapters in first person and third person, for example – but they really are as rare as hen's teeth. By now, as a writer, you will have discovered a slight preference for using one or the other, and that's something that's worthy of consideration when making your choice. For me, as an example, it was easy. I'd written around a hundred short stories by the time I attempted a novel and though I wrote in first and third, first was my favourite, my go-to form. If there was no reason for me to use third person, for the most part, I didn't. I loved the intimacy of becoming my protagonist. Though it does have its limitations: if you write in first person, the only viewpoint the reader shares is that of your viewpoint character, obviously.

Third is different – or at least can be. There are novels written in third person, because that's the author's choice, but where there is still only one viewpoint present. But using third person means you can explore several viewpoints, and have things happen that your main viewpoint character isn't privy to, which for some plots is obviously essential.

So think: whose story is it that you're telling? You will need a strong central protagonist to take readers on this journey, and it's with this character that they will be identifying, and through their eyes that they see the story unfolding. At this point you have a choice of first or third.

Then think further: are there any other characters whose voices need to be heard in your novel, as opposed to being seen only through your main protagonist's eyes? Other key characters you need the reader to relate to one-on-one, as opposed to just being viewed through the filter of your first protagonist's eyes? If so, you will need to use more than one viewpoint, which means, in almost all cases, writing in third person. This also applies, remember, if your plot needs to contain chapters or scenes in which your main protagonist isn't present.

Characters

We'll look more closely at characters in the next section, but one of the first things you should be doing at this very early stage is getting to know the person or persons central to your story. You'll be spending a lot of time with them over the coming weeks and months, and if they're to serve your purpose (i.e. be the sort of people legions of readers want to spend time with too) it's crucial that you know what makes them tick.

So think: what do you already know about them? Jot down anything you like – any random thought about what they look like, what drives them, how they speak, what they love or hate – and keep adding all the time to your list. Knowing your main characters well before you start is not an optional extra. You need to know them intimately if you are to make a half-decent job of having them respond realistically to all the dramas and traumas with which you plan on testing their mettle.

Focussing more tightly, what aspect(s) of their character (informed by their growing backstory) are going to be tested/challenged/changed as a result of their journey? What character trait or flaw, or misconception about something, is going to be addressed and changed by events? Can you readily sum up your main characters' main personality attributes? If so, what are they, and how do they impact on the theme and plot? A character that is quick to lose their temper, for example, will make for very different scenes and consequences than one with a slow fuse and a calm, tolerant soul.

Plot

Plot is what happens in your story in order to illustrate the theme of your novel. Keep that in mind. Learn it as a mantra. That way you will be less inclined to put anything in there that doesn't work towards achieving that aim. Novels that lose sight of this are the ones described as 'meandering', 'slow', and the always damning 'saggy in the middle'. They fail to make the reader turn pages.

Plotting is a difficult process to describe, since, for so many writers, it tends to be so organic. Again, we'll come back to it, but your initial thoughts should at least include a couple of pointers; where you're going to start, where you plan to end, how you're going to get there. Use a simple 'boy meets girl/gets girl/loses girl/gets girl back again' formula if you like. This is just an early overview that you can expand upon as you do your planning.

A thought: from time to time a student comes along to class and says 'but I don't know what the ending is, and I won't know till I get to it. And, anyway, I don't want to (they can tend to get a little chippy at this point) because it'll be no fun if I know how it ends!' And I get their point. *Up* to a point, anyway. Some argue that, since the process of creation is, almost by definition, one of discovery, there is merit in the 'start writing and see where it takes you' approach. Indeed, in terms of limbering up and planning, I even advocate it. There's nothing quite like the feeling that your mind is running away with you; a glorious torrent of ideas, counter ideas, bursts of inspiration all spewing forth, and that sense that your fingers can't fly at keyboard or A4 pad fast enough. Those are precious times, and you'd be mad not to milk them for all they're worth. Those are the times for which the proverbial 'notebook and pen to hand' were invented. But with the novel itself I would advocate extreme caution. If you don't know how and where your book ends I can't quite get my head round how you could possibly know how and where to start it. Remember, you're plotting a course between two points – one at the beginning and one at the end. Without both, you're adrift and if it *does* all pan out fine, it will be less by design than rare and happy accident. Which is a big risk. In an already risky career choice…

Major events/Key scenes

Do you have any of these in your head? If so, good. This is where the meat of the plotting comes in – how you start creating structure from the raw materials massing in your head. Once you have a handle on one – get that sense that you can properly begin to see it happening in your mind's eye – think about where it might fit into your timeline. Every time a potential scene (big, small, action-packed, romantic, contemplative, violent, heart-stopping, profound) comes to mind and persists in engaging your attention – if you can almost taste it, as part of that torrent of ideas' process – take the time to jot down every single detail and thought you can about it, even down to any dialogue you can hear your characters saying. It's all money in the bank you can cash later.

The beginning

What is your beginning? What is it about this event that makes it the starting point of a story? Think hard about where you begin your story, as a common mistake new writers make is to start too early, before the action starts to happen, in the mistaken belief that the readers need all the facts about everyone before they can 'get into' the story. 'In the middle of things' is a good rule of thumb. 'At the main character's conception, followed by a short précis of everything that happened to him (and his immediate family) before he got hit by the bus/bitten by the Rottweiler/stranded at the top of Everest without an anorak' is not. You can bring all that in while the immediate family are hanging around ITU, chatting about stuff, while waiting to see if he pulls through.

There's an authorly term that's been coined for 'in the middle of things', incidentally. It's **in medias res**, from the Latin. And a thought well worth keeping in, well, in medias res.

Step 1 Exercises

Is all about blurbs… This first exercise is to try and write one for your fledgling novel. Want to know what a blurb is? That's simple. Take a look at the back of any fiction paperback – go on, just grab one, or six, or twelve, at random – and you'll see what I mean. We'll return to blurbs later but having a stab at one now, for *your* book, will help to concentrate your mind.

Having said that, as, from Step 2 on, the exercises will be quite focussed and prescriptive, for one time only, if you don't want to do a blurb, that's okay. Since one of the core skills you'll need if you want to be a novelist is the ability to sit down and express yourself, via writing fiction, **on demand**, you might as well start practicing right away.

Yes, that's right. Pause in your reading and go and write something – anything. A chunk of your novel perhaps, a piece of description, some dialogue, a character study. The choice is yours.

Alternatively, you could write down the following:

Theme
Setting
Viewpoint
Characters
Plot
Major events
The beginning

And you could start.

Step 2 : Groundwork

As discussed in step one, a number of things need to be in place before you can start planning your novel to any degree, and the three we're going to look at more closely now are **Theme**, **Setting** and **Central Character(s)**.

Theme

In order for a novel to have broad appeal, it needs to explore a universal theme (or themes). This doesn't mean it should be bland, or dumbed down, or humdrum. Simply that it's peopled by characters who exhibit the sort of feelings many people have either experienced for themselves or can imagine experiencing at some point in their lives – either actual or fantasy.

For action-driven novels i.e. crime novels, adventure stories, thrillers (including psychological), and some fantasy, horror and sci-fi, these could include the triumph of good over evil, justice, retribution, fear and manipulation, abuse of power, and revenge. An example of this might be Michael Crichton's hugely successful *Jurassic Park*, the themes of which are as universal as they come; the rampage of modern science, the creation of monsters, people behaving badly, the results of untram-melled megalomania etc. Set against these are the staples of good over evil; the triumph of morality over naked ambition, the retribution of mother nature, and the bolt-on (which was somewhat over-egged in the movie, to my mind) of ambition being tempered and ultimately held to account by the best perspective-shifter there is: the love of children.

For feeling-driven novels i.e. relationship stories, romance, rom-com, and some sagas, these might include love in all its forms, betrayal, jealousy, courage, self-sacrifice, duty and loss. An example of this might be Helen Fielding's equally loved *Bridget Jones' Diary*, the themes of which speak to women everywhere; low self-esteem (not to mention poor or eccentric mothering) leading to self-destructive behaviour and poor relationship choices which (for this genre, anyway) are ultimately overcome through loving oneself, and as a result, being able to love and be loved. In another genre, obviously, they might be explored differently and less humorously; the universality of the experience means it's a popular one, with seemingly a zillion permutations.

Some novels – long family sagas, crime series with a strong central protagonist who has a series-spanning personal story, and complex fantasies spring to mind – there will be an overlap between 'action' and 'the mind' as story-drivers. This is also true of novels that document epic journeys. All these books tend to have the power to cross gender divides, which is why they are so commercially successful; P D James' Adam Dalgleish, for example, is as much thoughtful romantic hero as hard-nosed detective, and creations such as Lee Child's moral drifter, Jack Reacher, is a clever one: the women want him, the men want to be him.

An aside here; there's a commonly held perception that while most women will read fiction narrated by women *and* men, the reverse is, apparently, almost never true. Which is galling for women but no longer necessarily accurate. Female protagonists can and do break through that most persistent of barriers. Take Lisbeth Salander (and if you don't recognise the name go and Google it immediately!) because, hot on the heels of Miss Marple – such a pleasing image – she represents a thoroughly modern watershed in that respect.

Setting

As was touched on in step one, in choosing a setting, you need to consider both time and place. Is it an environment you know well? If not, can you do sufficient research to make it believable to the reader?

Do you know someone who works within it who could help and advise? If not a contemporary novel, when in history (or, indeed, the future) do you want to set it? More importantly, *why*?

This is important, as it will impact heavily on how much work you are going to need to do in terms of research. So consider carefully. Is the setting integral to the plot or incidental to it? To put it another way, do the location, time and environment impact on the actual storyline? Does the book actually *need* to be set there? If you had been the late Dick Francis, writing thrillers set in the world of horse racing, then, clearly, you'd have needed to know all about it. Similarly, if your theme involves the exploration of the human condition as affected by war, say, or famine, or other desperate situations that you might not have personally experienced, then you need to be prepared to do the groundwork. There are few things more irritating for a reader than coming across a factual error, because it contributes to breaking that unspoken bond between you – the reader's suspension of disbelief in your fiction. Remember at all times that while a novel's purpose is to explore a universal human truth or truths, the way it does that is by fabrication – telling *untruths*. Though seemingly insignificant, little lapses of care in creating your fictitious world can have the power to break that contract; that sense the reader feels of having entered another all too real world. (And they do – why else do people cry when reading books? Because it *feels* real. Which is what makes them care.) So think hard about where and then WHY you want to set yours where and when you do.

Incidentally, location and setting, above most other variables, are most subject to the vagaries of fashion. At the turn of the century, for instance, you might have noticed that books about Asian minority groups in Britain became popular, then were superseded by a new interest in eastern Europeans. With big social changes ongoing, who knows what will come next? Similarly, vampires made a big comeback a few years ago, werewolves and angels are intwermittently in vogue, and last I heard, there was a rumbling that trolls (a generally maligned lot) might be the next mythical folk up for a PR makeover. I personally wouldn't bank on it, however. My money is now on Pandemic-fic. Isn't yours?

One thing I would add, all the above notwithstanding, is that you should remember how long it takes to get a book published, and to resist the urge to write about something currently fashionable just because you think it will stand a better chance of being published. It won't. In fact, the reverse is probably true – because even with the best will in the world, and a following wind, it will take a year for you to write it, a good few months or more to find an agent, and that agent – unless you are simply brilliant or very lucky – several more to find a publisher to offer you a deal for it. It will then take a year for them to get the thing in shops and who knows what the idea *du jour* will be by then? You can bet your life it will no longer be the one that was oh-so popular when you first began. Don't, then, pick a setting because you think it's of the moment. Pick one that works for *you*, every time.

(Incidentally, if what works for you just happens to be fashionable as you're writing, try not to worry about that either. The truth is that if you write YOUR book, in YOUR voice, rather than trying to bend to what you perceive to be popular, it will be a far better, more original book.)

Central Character

Every novel has at least one central character, through whose eyes we see the story unfold. Sometimes there are two – such as in a 'his and hers' type narrative, or where there's a detective and a sidekick – and sometimes three; the 'three women with interlinking stories' approach is a staple of both rom coms and relationship tales. The important thing is to never lose sight of the fact that it is they – and NOT you – who are relating the tale, and whose point of view you are trying to get across.

Creating realistic characters, therefore, is essential, and a good way to think about approaching the job is to think in terms of a character's depth. If a character in a short story is essentially a snapshot of a real person (most short stories tend to have a very tight focus, of course) then a character in a novel is more like the collection of cine-films or videos amassed over their lifetime. This being so, you need to create a **backstory** for them. Most of this will never actually appear in your novel (indeed, it shouldn't unless it impacts on the plot) but it needs to be clear in your head as you write in order that your character's motivations and responses to adversity ring true.

A good start point is to **marry up your theme and your protagonist (s)**, which can be done by first establishing the latter's 'good' traits and 'bad' traits so as to serve your requirements for the former. For example, if your theme is about being courageous and true to oneself, then your protagonist must start the book *not* being so, in order for them to become so as a result of their journey. They need to be recognizably, and sympathetically, flawed in this regard because it's that sense of recognition (ah, yes, I remember feeling like that myself) that creates the sympathy (so I know just how *they* feel). No, it's not rocket science, but it does require emotional intelligence to do this. And empathy. To be a novelist is to display empathy for your fellow human – if you don't, then that connection won't happen.

So, since you're playing God, think about creating characters with a clear sense of purpose. Give them personalities and idiosyncrasies that suit your needs. Say your theme is about self-determination – having the courage to pursue your own path. To maximize the impact of the 'hero's journey' to a place where they're able to do that, you need to provide contrast by having them start on that journey in a place where it's an observable flaw. Perhaps they are used to subjugating their needs to those of others (an eldest sibling, for example, or domineering parent) or someone who will readily bend their will to another. Conversely, if your theme is about learning humility and what matters in life, then your character, perhaps damaged and lacking empathy as the result of an unhappy childhood, could be someone who starts their journey as something of a tyrant; one who behaves badly in the pursuit of an ambition.

It's probably more important than you might realise that you have this strong sense of purpose from the outset. You are not just amassing a lot of words, you are creating a *whole* world; one in which to explore something that's of sufficient interest to your fellow human that they want to join you on the adventure you're going to stage there. And that means it needs resonance – the reader *must* care about the outcome. And that happens, for the most part, because they get to know a bunch of wholly fictional people who, for the duration of the story, act in ways that feel absolutely real. Yes, there's scene setting, and writing style and a flair for creating tension, but it's the depth and resonance of your characters which does the real work in this regard.

Creating characters is not difficult or complicated, and I'm making the assumption that, having reached a point where you intend to write a novel, you know the basic process of invention. Indeed, characters, in a lot of cases, invent themselves in your subconscious, rather like the drift of wildflowers that emerges from a casual sowing of seed that has the benefit of being strewn on fertile ground. Characters are everywhere, and if they haven't already come to you almost fully formed (some writers have been known to simply pluck them from their immediate locale – though composites, particularly in the case of unsympathetic characters, are generally safer from a peace, harmony and no-litigation perspective) then the demands of your fledgling story should help suggest what sort of people they need to be. Remember, at this stage (if not every stage) you are in complete control. Mould them carefully so that, together, they will do their work well.

There is, however, one important thing to bear in mind about your characters. That you will never be in a position (unless you intend to write from the point of view of God, or some other omnipotent being) to describe them objectively. Think hard about this, however counter-intuitive it seems.

And consider this. The following extracts come from a book by the talented (and hugely successful) Author, Sarah Harrison, whose 1995 handbook *How to Write a Blockbuster* was of my early fiction writing bibles, and the book I credit with putting me in the perfect mental place to take the leap and begin writing my first novel.

Take a look at the three character descriptions below:

1. *'Victoria was small and slim. She had a pale, heart-shaped face with wide-set grey eyes and a straight nose above full lips. She wore no make up or jewellery and her dark hair was tied*

smoothly back. Her suit was plain and well tailored, her shoes had only a low heel and her nails were cut short and unpolished. She was too sober-looking to be pretty but there was something quietly attractive about her.'

2. *'Gabrielle followed his {the man she was with's} gaze and saw Victoria. Good God – this was her rival, the woman she'd come to fear? This small, plain, painfully neat person, with her hair scraped back and her serviceable suit and her sensible, well-polished shoes? This unremarkable little body with unplucked eyebrows, who was currently turning her unadorned face upward to be kissed by the richest man in the room…'*

3. *'He stared, but not only from curiosity. She was the most powerful woman in the room and she demonstrated it by her refusal to accept the conventions of the occasion. Amongst the couture clothes and big hair, the show-off jewellery and expensively honed bodies, her quiet appearance shrieked for attention. And besides, Guy, accustomed to notice such things, took in a short, deeply grooved upper lip, an arrogantly unblinking gaze, slender ankles and, beneath that school teacher's suit, a lissome waist and a bosom to die for – probably, he thought, clothed in snow-white cotton underwear…'*

In her book, Sarah explains in detail how these descriptions differ, and I hope you can see, just from reading them, what a world of possibilities exists for you as an author, once you start exploring the many ways in which you can bring characters to life on the page. Here we have, in 1. what could be construed as a workaday, objective, visual description, in 2. The description of a woman as seen through the eyes of a love-rival and finally, in 3. Another take on Victoria – by a man who finds her deeply attractive.

Take a moment to consider the ways in which these three descriptions differ and, having done so, think too about another thing that's true of them – that the second two don't only give up some facts about Victoria – they give us insights into the characters who are doing the describing, too.

What I hope you've taken from this, as I did when I first read it, is an elegant and important truth. That **all the characters in your novel will be _viewed through the eyes of other characters_, which will make almost all of your descriptions _sub_jective.** Your protagonists have only two modes of expression – they are either seen through their own eyes ('I have the most hateful, unmanageable, straw-textured mass of hair, and I can never do anything with it'), or through the eyes of other viewpoint characters ('she was stunningly beautiful; a free spirit. Ethereal. Her hair, a mass of waves that might grace a Grecian goddess….). A tad whimsical, but I hope you get the gist. Also remember that non-viewpoint characters – i.e. those whose thoughts the reader is not privy to – can also have input in describing other characters (just as they can have input into developing your plot and imparting key information – more of which later). They perform this function through dialogue.

To sum up, every character will bring their own prejudices, tastes and preoccupations to their worldview, and this will influence how they perceive others. **Keep this in mind as you are writing; how we are seen will always depend on who's seeing.**

One, two, three…

Though I've listed Theme, Character and Setting in a certain order, it really doesn't matter how they're arrived at. Sometimes a character will imprint him or herself on your consciousness in much the same way a beguiling new friend might, suggesting a possible theme in the process. At other times, a setting you know well, and which excites you, will prove too compelling to ignore (there are doubtless ex-bankers, even now, who are sharpening their pencils, not to mention a couple of retired football alumni).

Themes, too, have a habit of arousing our passions; it might be the current obsession with sex and physical beauty, or the divorce statistics, or knife crime, or religious tensions, or the ramifications of stem cell research. The only constant is that once you have all three in place, you've laid the foundations on which everything else will be built. Start writing in earnest without a clear sense of all of them and you risk heading up an awful lot of blind alleys. (Metaphor, by the way, in week six…)

Step 2 Exercise

This is an exercise about developing character, based on what you've read above, so you can have a go at putting what you've learned into practice. It comes in three parts and the aim is to make you think: there is, of course, a place in fiction for straightforward, objective character description but your prose will have much more depth if you are constantly mindful of just how much opportunity for characterization you really have. .

First of all, look at the three pictures below, which, for ease of understanding are, left to right, A, B and C.

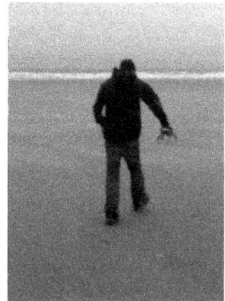

The first task is to write a couple of hundred words about each of them, as if they were describing themselves. You can write in first or third person, but the point of view must be theirs; as if they were looking in a mirror and describing themselves.

The second task is to have character A write a description of character B, as if she and he are already well acquainted. How and why is up to you but try to keep in mind as you write what you've already established about character A, as well as their personal take on character B.

The third task is to bring character C into the equation. Give him some sort of axe to grind about the relationship between characters A and B. Again, the 'what' part is up to you; the important thing is to create contrast and, again, illuminate both describer and describees.

Step 3 : Making an entrance

As an unpublished writer one of the first hurdles you'll encounter is that there's a sizeable chance that potential readers of your Great Work will not, in fact, get a chance to read it. This is because you will first have to get representation by an agent, and agents (being busy, and often disinclined to benevolence) make a speciality of not reading further than the first page. My own agent, for instance, will not even consider reading a manuscript if the first page is any of the following:

Hand written
Littered with punctuation errors and spelling mistakes
Not written in half-decent, publishable English
Clearly of a genre that they don't handle
Boring

Though we'll deal with the top four later in the course (all of which are unforgivable but happen much more than you might imagine), the last is something you need to address early because having a first page (and, it goes without saying, a first chapter) that excites interest is essential to your novel's success.

What constitutes 'exciting' is dependent upon personal taste, obviously, but one thing that unites almost all successful novels, whatever genre, is that they have a beginning which compels the reader to read on.

There are a few notable exceptions to this, of course. There is a class of novel – often one which attains fame long after it is first published – which becomes a word of mouth success, involving words along the lines of 'the beginning is pretty turgid, but it eventually gets going, so stick with it. By the end I really couldn't put it down…' This often happens with books that make a good showing at the Man Booker, because, similarly, there is a class of reader who does not feel they've earned their literary spurs unless they've 'persevered' with a 'challenging' read. Most novelists, however, if quizzed about their intentions, would admit that what they'd like is for readers to like both end *and* beginning, and hopefully everything else in between. They also often lament – very often straight after winning the Man Booker – that thirty seven agents and a further twenty three publishers all turned them away in the first instance….

So, all other things being equal (which they aren't) it mostly pays to attempt to start in the middle of things – In *medias res*, as the Greek (and pretentious creative writing tutors) tend to have it. Unfortunately, the commonest mistake new writers seem to make is to completely ignore that, believing that it's first necessary to set out one's stall. They therefore put all their energies into introducing their characters, in much the same way a 1970s TV chef might introduce their little glass bowls of ingredients, with the result that they begin their novels with a lengthy, and mostly tedious, and often contrived, preamble. In the very worst cases, this exercise runs to a whole chapter that reads more like a seed catalogue than a story. The word preamble, take note, contains the word 'amble' within it, which should remind you why you should avoid it.

Two key things, therefore, to remember:

Most novels by novice writers are improved immeasurably by simply having chapters one and two swapped around. Remember, something BIG needs to happen to your principal characters, pretty much immediately, in order for us to feel interested enough in them to want to know why and how they got to where they got. i.e. your story must start *with* the story. If you sit down to a meal you want to dive straight in and eat it; not sit watching it cool as the chef spends twenty minutes sitting at the table with you, describing where they sourced the ethically reared pig.

As the cliché so often has it – always, *always* start in the middle of things. As I've already said, make *In medias res* your mantra.

At this stage, unless you are a confirmed 'start writing anything and see where it might take you' sort of writer (in which case, all these pointers – and, indeed, lessons – won't apply) it's probably useful to think of another major event in your novel i.e. the place where you want it to end. This is of much more importance than you might think. And that's because unless you are one of a very small minority (perhaps sitting in the same room as all those 107 year old 60-a -day smokers we always hear about) the strength of your ending will depend, in large part, on the contrast with how things started out.

To use a simple example, Wimbledon Champion is a fine thing to achieve, whatever the circumstances around it. But a Wimbledon champion who was champion last year, and the year before, and had a steady rise up the rankings since a privileged and sporty childhood, is a far less interesting happening, in a storytelling sense, than one who came out of nowhere, had an inauspicious, tennis academy-free beginning and had no idea of the extent of their talent. And even better, in storytelling terms, is if that champion-to-be, on their way to fame and glory, had some pretty sticky, life-changing, dramatic things happen – nearly losing their life, say, or succumbing to some of what the writing guru Ronald Tobias (see reading list) would call a period of 'Wretched Excess.'

In short, you need contrast: you need an enthralling journey to take place. And the place to start illustrating the scope of that journey is in the sense of drama, and therefore empathy, you invoke on that first page. Yes, you might well change your end point once you're travelling along the road to it, but for now, at least, some sense of the destination you're intending to get to is a bit of a must-have for most.

Hopefully, this is something you *will* have because a) you already thought about the theme of your story, b) you already know your setting and lead players fairly intimately and c) have some sense of the point of your tale i.e. how those players are going to interact with one another and what the consequences of those interactions are going to be, which… pause for breath… will illustrate that theme.

I use two analogies – you might prefer another. I see the emerging structure of my novels as either a tube line (or any other kind of transport network) or a watercolour painting, and sometimes both. If the former, and my start point is a dramatic happening at London Paddington, then I'll plot my end point (for argument and irony's sake, Waterloo), and then start to identify all the underground stations in the form of a route that will get me from A to B.

Similarly, if you want to think in terms of an artwork, your start and end points, plus those major events you already know are going to feature, are like the pencil marks you make before you bring out your palette; the bare bones of the story, ready to be fleshed out.

About now, of course, sick of drowning in so many mixed metaphors, you might like to commit real things – real events; real *scenes* – to paper (or screen, or file card, or notebook, or whatever). Hopefully, being a creative writer, you will feel creative about this project, and already have a number of such scenes in mind – even, if you are like me, whole passages of dialogue within them. In which case, commit them to paper or screen.

What you'll have, at the end of this process, it's hoped, is what's known in writing circles as your 'Narrative Arc', which is mostly just a pretentious way of saying 'story' or 'plot', but you'll be surprised by how readily, once you've embraced the concept, you'll get a feel for a narrative arc that feels right.

In the meantime, what you have is the basis of an outline that will hopefully, now you've given it substance, do what it needs to do – begin to grow.

Step 3 Exercise

News headlines can often provide a rich source of inspiration, since they can spark your fiction writer's mind into action so readily. That 'whaattt?' response we have when we read an intriguing headline is one we should nurture and develop. How did *that* come about? What on *earth* is the back story? Could something so bizarre *really* have happened? What sort of person would *do* such a thing? Do I even *believe* that? There *has* to be more to this. And so on.

Collecting headlines is a pastime you might want to adopt; either in your head or in a file, it doesn't matter. What matters is that you are amassing a creative resource. Real life stories are one of our most precious resources – you could even argue that they comprise the major part of our stock of raw materials, since human interaction is the bedrock on which all fiction is built.

They can also, on occasion, provide a valuable spur to creation, or missing link. The news clip below was one I spotted while travelling home on a flight from Berlin. At this point, I had a heroine, a hero, and a loose sketch of a story, but what I needed was something which would suddenly – and also slightly catastrophically – transplant my hapless heroine deep into enemy territory (in this case, upper middle class suburbia). This event, once re-sited to a terraced south London street, seemed just the thing. That it was a newsworthy happening was actually crucial to my plot.

Germany
Excavator hits WW2 bomb at NRW site

An excavator struck an unexploded American WW2 bomb on Friday at the site of the former Huttengelande on Strasse am Walzwerk, Hattingen, the excavator operator and 16 others were injured. The blast from the 250-Kg bomb which lay half-a-metre underground saw substantial damage within a 300 metre radius, with some fragments being detected as far as 1,500 metres away. 20th September 2008.

Exercise: Taking any headline that grabs you (perhaps even the one above) as your inspiration, have a go at penning an immediately engaging, arresting, and truly memorable (etc etc) hypothetical first page of a novel.

Step 4 : Plotting and Planning

Hopefully, by, now, with your hypothetical novel, you will have some ideas in your head concerning a number of variables;

Theme, central characters, setting and basic story

Whose story it is and the style in which you plan to tell it i.e. choice of first or third person (or some variation on that theme, if you feel courageous) and who your viewpoint character or characters are going to be.

Some idea of where the story is going to end, and, provisionally at least, how it's going to get there.

It's important to recognise (and not fret about) the fact that none of these variables are set in stone. Indeed, you might have several options still for any of the above details, in which case, don't try to whittle them down artificially. As you continue to flesh out the bare bones of your plot, you will find those that work will bubble naturally to the surface while those that don't either quietly disappear from your thought processes, morph into some other, more workable set of variables, or become obviously untenable as ideas.

The central thing at this stage is to start thinking in a loosely linear fashion, starting with the words 'beginning', 'middle' and 'end', if you like, but all the time filling in the gaps. What you are aiming to achieve at the end of the process is the basis of your chapter by chapter outline.

My books invariably tend to run to about 30 chapters of around 3,000 words each. I don't know why that is, it just is. And it holds broadly true for all the genres I've written in. For others, the chapter count can be double that. The point to note here is that there is no right or wrong; the number of chapters isn't nearly as important as the overall word count of your book.

On the whole, and this is true of both fiction and narrative non-fiction, size does tend to matter. There is a reason why the books in any given bookshop look similar, size wise, and it's because we seem to have a clear sense of how big a physical book should be. *Why* that's happened is another question, for another book, perhaps, at another time, but in the physical world (and as I write, most budding authors still want to see their work there) anything less than about 70,000 will feel too short and anything longer than, say, 150,000, too long.

Again, how long you make your novel is entirely up to you. Perhaps nothing less than a weighty one thousand pages will do. High art (and high literature) make their own rules, every time. And, as a reader, I love nothing more than a really long book. But be aware that in genre fiction – crime novels, for example – weighty thousand page tomes are rare beasts. I'd also counsel further thought if your first full length novel looks like coming in at anything under sixty thousand words. It might find an audience, but, to most editors, it's not going to be long enough – you'll even find approximate wordcounts specified in publishing contracts. Again, I don't know why it is, it just is. Just as a movie tends to always be longer than an hour and very rarely any longer than three.

All of which is easy for me to say, but how do you know at this stage how long your novel is likely to be? How on earth can you know? You've never done this before. The answer is simpler than you think. You'll know instinctively, because you read novels all the time and – again, this doesn't apply if you are seriously experimental – you'll have a feel for how much action is generally contained between the covers of the kind of book you want to write. And if you make a plan, breaking it down into chunks, and then chapters, you'll have a feel for whether yours contains sufficient.

Now is where you are really, properly limbering up the Big Task Ahead – once your plan is in place in a form you feel happy with, there will be really no reason why you shouldn't start writing, and, hopefully, you will already be itching to get going, even if you do find yourself running around doing displacement activities as an art form, just to put off that life-changing moment. Never, at this stage, be reticent about writing down any lines of thought, bits of dialogue, descriptive details and so on – look upon these, as I know I have said before, as all so much money in the bank.

The original planning document for my 2005 novel, *Wild About Harry*, (written under my pseudonym, Daisy Jordan) ran to almost 10,000 words, and if you visit my website, you can see it for yourself. I mention it not because it's the best way, I hasten to add. It was just *my* way at the time, and served me well. And it's there because it's an example of the creative process in action – the flights of ideas, the sudden eureka moments about characters and/or action, the snippets of dialogue that seemed too precious not to be noted down right away – and, more importantly, it resulted in a published novel, so the relationship between the planning and the final book can be seen. Feel free to glance at it, and take from it what you will.

Incidentally, I took my own advice when, in 2018, I branched out into a completely different genre. With my 2020 psychological thriller, *Can You See Me?*, (another pseudonym, this time Lynne Lee) I felt as much the rookie as I did when I penned my first rom com 20 years earlier. Perhaps more so – these are books that are invariably *very* twisty, requiring the author to keep multiple thought-balls in the air. So, belt and braces, before I wrote so much as a word, I amassed not only my traditional 10,000 word outline, but also a 5000 word backstory (i.e. what *really* happened), a detailed timeline, and a further 4000 words in the shape of character studies – all of which I referred to, and added to, again and again.

As I say, there is no right way. Only your way. Mine seems always to be a thought process – one that continues right through the actual writing – that starts with the words 'novel # notes' in a file, and grows organically as each new thought not only adds to the total, but also causes me to expand, or modify, or expunge earlier thoughts. This might not be a method that works for you visually, but whatever your own choice of system – pictures, index cards, a wall chart, a flow diagram – the basic process of construction will be fundamentally similar; you will have a start point, an end point (or choice of end points, obviously) plus a number of key scenes that will link those two points. You will then start the process of linking each link point, so creating a great number of possible scenes, which will eventually, singly, or in small groupings, create chapters.

Bear in mind that the choice of chapters shouldn't be random (more on chapters shortly), and that they don't have to be of uniform length. Instead, think of each chapter end as a natural pause to draw breath; for the reader to assimilate and take in all the new developments they've just read. And remember, in itself, the choice of end point for a chapter is important.

By choosing to end a chapter where you do, you are indicating that something particularly important has happened which you expect the reader to keep in mind as they read on.

You also need to keep a couple of things in mind yourself;

That, in order to keep reading, your reader has to care; both about the characters you're introducing them to (which means they need to be both sympathetic, and with recognisable motivations) and also that the story is one that's worth telling – a gentle account of pleasant exchanges between happy, well-adjusted people has no place in fiction, so if you find this happening in your narrative, cause trouble for them right away. The only real exception to this rule is when you start writing 'The End' immediately following that juncture. Think in terms of conflict at all times. An easy way is to keep asking yourself the question 'what does my character want and how are they going to get it? What's stopping them from getting it? Why and how?

The importance of creating suspense. The only reason a reader keeps reading a book is because *they want to know what's going to happen next.* **Your main job as a storyteller is to pose questions and delay answering them** – to keep that sense of excited expectation at full throttle, not just in terms of them wanting to know the ending (if that were the case you could just give them the synopsis to read) but also at all the junctures of expectation along the way. At every point possible, make them wait. **There shouldn't be a chapter that doesn't end on a note that makes them anxious to turn the page and read the next one**. If the lovers are about to kiss, interrupt them. If the cop's about to catch the villain, have him suddenly escape. **Think shocks and surprises and delayed gratification. I really can't emphasise this enough.**

And so to some bullet points about plotting and planning. First up, to get you thinking about plots and subplots…

Key Points about Plotting : a tick list

As Picasso said (and yes, I do know he was talking about art – it matters little) you need to learn the rules in order to know how to break them. Here, in no particular order, are a few of my personal must dos, with some credit to the incomparable Ronald B Tobias, whose wisdoms about storytelling taught me such a lot…

1. Make tension fuel your plot.
2. Create tension through opposition by creating a worthy antagonist or antagonists: this can mean a person – e.g. Moriarty, a place – e.g. Tara, the ranch in Gone With the Wind, or a thing – e.g. alcoholism.
3. Ensure tension grows as you go along – increase the overall tension of the wider story by introducing smaller tensions along the way.

4. Make **change** the point of your story.

5. If and when something happens in your story, make sure it's important – make sure there is a reason. Otherwise, cut it. Murder both your stylistic darlings and your meandering ones.

6. Always make the causal look casual. Avoid clunks.

7. Have your main character perform the main action in the climax. Remember – action, **not** reaction.

8. Luck, chance, fate, destiny. None of these are plot devices. Avoid them. Coincidence is fine to bring your characters together in the **beginning**, but has no place in your storytelling once you've begun.

9. *Deus ex machina*. Look this up. Essentially, never use an artificial contrivance of any sort (the invention of an unexpected character/object or event) to solve an intractable plot problem. Everything must happen for a reason.

Subplots exist to:

serve the needs of the main plot

throw new light on an event in the main plot

provide a 'pause' to heighten tension, after a key moment in the main plot

add to characterisation by revealing the protagonists in different relationships

add richness and verisimilitude to your portrayal of 'real' life

provide the main protagonist with a moral 'steer' to help them reach a decision

enable you to explore the theme of your novel from another angle

Once you have a plot in place, at some point you'll need to start thinking about chapters, of course – where to start them, where to end them, what they are. So, second up, here are some further chapter thoughts.

Chapters – a do and don't list

Below are some do, don't and general notes about creating chapters within your fiction, none of which are to be taken as gospel, obviously, but all of which have proved useful to some writer, working on some book, at some time…

Chapter lengths vary according to genre and country. In the UK, an average paperback might be 75 thousand words long, and the average chapter might be around 3 thousand. Mine mostly are. Yours might deviate somewhat. Genrewise, action thrillers and police procedurals tend to have shorter chapters, while those in romance, sci-fi and sagas tend to be longer.

Pace varies too. Thrillers and crime again seem to demand a faster, more dialogue-heavy read, while the other genres tend to a more leisurely, more descriptive style. Rom-coms and contemporary comedy sit firmly in the middle.

A chapter should almost always end on something meaningful: a cliffhanger/ a question/an important declaration/reflection/decision.

Alternatively, it can end slap-bang in the *middle* of the slap, or, indeed, the bang.

A chapter should never just peter out. (Unless you have a character in it, called Peter, who is leaving.)

A chapter will often centre on a small number of related scenes. Think 'this chapter is mostly about…'

Remember that a chapter is usually bigger than a single scene (except as described below) and will also involve all the aspects that surround it; motivation, confrontation, consequences…

You should never change viewpoint mid-scene UNLESS you use a line break. It's fine to include several scenes in a chapter, in order to include different viewpoints, as long as they flow naturally one to the other.

A good way to heighten suspense is to vary the lengths of your chapters. Something action packed is often best served short and sharp, while emotional watershed conversations can strettttch.

Try to vary the way you start chapters. Start some with action, some with reflection, some with dialogue.

Likewise, vary the way you end them.

Take the reader away from the action from time to time to heighten anticipation. Remember – delay gratification for maximum unputdownability. Follow a scene that ends on a cliff-hanger by a diversion to a chapter about a sub-plot before rejoining the action in the next chapter.

Make sure your viewpoint and crucial adversarial characters are all introduced early on, so that your reader knows who to support or otherwise.

Do not introduce new integral characters 2/3rds of the way into the narrative, unless you are writing a long, multi generational saga.

Tie up your main subplot in your penultimate chapter. Do not muddy the final chapter with any unnecessary side-issues.

Head your chapters with Chapter…. and then the number, written in numerals. Don't give your chapters titles or descriptions or any other embellishments unless you have a good reason for doing so. They have a tendency to create unnecessary demands on your writing, as you try to 'theme' them artificially, or bend them into shape. And, remember, if some theme that lends itself to subtitling emerges all by itself, then it deserves to be there, and you can always add them later.

Don't artificially create chapters to fill in boxes on a grid. Remember, starting on Jan 1st and ending on Dec 31st has already been done. A lot. As has 'a dead lover leaving a series of letters for the bereaved to find every month'. Try and let your story stand unsupported.

33

Similarly, don't artificially form bridges between scenes. If you find yourself marooned on the bank with no way across, you need to go back to your outline.

If you reach a point where you're unsure how best to chop your narrative into chapters, don't be afraid to just keep on writing and sort the division out later. But don't start off like that unless it's already worked for you, because you *do* need chapters, and if you have to add them artificially, you will make a lot of work for yourself. Try to think like a reader.

Read in your chosen genre, and do it as a writer. Analyse how other writers make it work.

Remember, it's far easier to write a narrative if you already have a plan in place. So try to plan your chapters at the outset.

And finally...

A short (ish) note on headhopping

This is one of those proverbial 'hot potatoes' that come up intermittently and get inspected and discussed as a technique – most rigorously, I tend to find, in online forums. The term 'headhopping' refers to writing in which the author includes the thought processes of more than one character within a single scene. It's not to be confused with having different points of view (POVs) within your novel. If you write in the third person you will probably have several POVs included within it – that's normal practice and it's use is universal, because it's a useful, and therefore popular, device.

The most usual way of moving between viewpoints is to do so either by writing different chapters from different characters' POVs, or switching viewpoints when you switch scenes (usually denoted by a line break – more of which later on). Headhopping is different. Headhopping involves including the thoughts of different characters *within* scenes.

For example...

'Matt, you've had way too much to drink already this evening,' said Julia. She felt a familiar sense of desolation wash over her as she observed his halting steps and hooded gaze. His acid breath was eddying around her face and she winced. Could any man be less appealing, ever?

'You know what?' Matt replied. 'You can just go take a running jump, Jules. You know nothing about what I've been going through. Nothing!' He swung the gin bottle, causing a spray of liquid to arc into the air between them. *Good*, he thought. *Serve her right.* He was this close to smashing the thing over her pretty head. Not so pretty then, huh? Not at *all*.

Apart from it being 'not the norm' and so can jar as a result of its unfamiliarity to the average reader, the problem I have with headhopping is that it leaves the reader unclear as to who they should be rooting for. Yes, in a multi POV novel they might be rooting for more than one character, obviously, but in real life, at any given time, we're only privy to one point of view – our own. The same should, to my mind, apply in fiction too. Part of creating good fiction is the creation of sympathetic, rounded characters and we achieve this by stepping inside their heads and going on their journey with them, observing their thoughts and feelings as they interact with friend or foe. If you headhop you are diluting this process, and risk creating a sense of detachment in the reader; rather than feeling close to the one protagonist they are currently privileged to get inside the mind of, they become more like an observer – witnessing a bunch of characters but not getting so involved, as they don't have that emotional closeness that develops while travelling intimately with just the one person.

Some argue that as we now live in the time of film and television that having that all-seeing eye is beginning to feel more natural. I disagree. Though authors like Martina Cole have managed to headhop successfully, they are, and continue to be, in the minority. And for good reason. A book is not a film. It's a different art form. With different rules. So feel free to headhop, if you have a passion for doing so, but always bear in mind the above note of caution.

Step 4 exercise

Getting into the habit of writing taut, dramatic scenes is a very important skill if you want to keep a reader interested through many, many thousands of words of story. You therefore need to approach every single page of your novel with a critical, impatient eye. Remember that, in all but one case, your reader isn't your mother, and therefore doesn't care a jot about hurting your feelings. If they're bored for any length of time, they'll stop reading your book.

Exercise: Stations are great devices, aren't they? As are airports, and bus depots, and cruise-liner docks. So many stories arise from the every day business of people coming and going, parting and reuniting, weeping and smiling, feeling scared and relieved.

First up, choose a couple of characters from the photograph on the right, then, using the picture as both the setting and the inspiration for a fictional encounter, write a short scene which would sit well at the end of a chapter, taking in account of the importance of both **conflict** and **suspense** and, ideally, ending with a **cliffhanger**…

Step 5 : Dialogue

I am passionate about dialogue. Whether I'm use it sparingly, as a condiment, to add piquancy or bite, or have a field day and make the star of the show, I cannot imagine being a writer if it wasn't in the mix. Dialogue equals people communicating with one another, and since we can't read other people's minds (and neither can our viewpoint characters, remember), it's the best tool we have with which to do this. We can conjecture about other people, and make all sorts of assumptions, but it's only when we speak to them that we really get to know them.

The trick with writing good dialogue is to make it sound completely natural, despite it being nothing like natural speech at all. If you transcribe real conversation you'll find it is peppered with ums and ers, full of instances of people talking over each other, starting but not finishing trains of thought, rambling and not answering one another's questions. In short, real dialogue refuses to observe all the rules we hold as standard in fiction.

Fictional dialogue, in other words, behaves itself. Apart from interruptions – which work well to add tension and atmosphere – what you read on the page simply doesn't happen in real life. Fictional dialogue, by common consent, is a chimera.

As with the underwater effort we don't see as a swan glides across a body of water, good dialogue is hard to spot simply by virtue of the fact that, if done well, it doesn't even register as such; you don't consciously notice the punctuation at all, much less the alternate speeches, the feeding in of vital information, the crafty bits of characterization and scene setting. Poor dialogue, on the other hand, screams out its inadequacies. It actually brings you up short.

It's perhaps not surprising that dialogue is hard, when you think about it, because it has such a great deal to do. Moreover, of all the aspects of fiction writing it's the least amenable to being stylish and idiosyncratic. Where beautiful style can sometimes make up for lack of characterization, and fabulous characters compensate for a somewhat shaky plot, dialogue takes no prisoners. Get it wrong and it can not only drag a book down, it can even tend a reader towards violence. It doesn't flow, it doesn't work. End of story.

Dialogue – sorry to hammer it home – is the lifeblood of almost all genres of fiction. Editors often refer to it as providing the 'white space' on a novel's pages; what sets it apart as a narrative, a story, as opposed to any other kind of book. Without that white space, a book can feel sluggish and text book-like, even before you start to read the words.

It is with dialogue, therefore, more than any other component of the craft, that the words 'show, don't tell' really come into their own. And in short fiction particularly, your dialogue needs clout, as you have so little space for it to do all the things I keep reminding you it needs to do.

So what are they? Well, in summary, as follows:

To bring your story to life:

Dialogue is where your characters really start making that connection with the reader. Until they speak, all we know of them is what the viewpoint character **tells** us, and what we infer from their observed actions – when they speak, you can really **show** the reader what they're like.

To move the action along:

Unless your story takes the form of a reflective monologue, at some point your characters need to begin interacting, and in most cases, speaking to one another when they do. In their words to one another they will start revealing the story.

To incorporate backstory and any vital off-stage information:

But the best dialogue does this so cleverly and stealthily, that the reader won't really even notice it happening. If they do, it hasn't been done quite well enough.

To display character and to differentiate between characters:

People change how they speak according to whom they are speaking. Most people will speak differently to a small child, a superior at work, an elderly lady, an aggressive customer…. Paradoxically, most people also have very set speech patterns. Phrasing statements as questions, using an idiosyncratic form of words, are interrupters, or exclaimers, or apologists… Also think accents, colloquialisms, preferred profanities, verbal tics.

To create atmosphere and tension:

Nothing beats dialogue for racking up the tension – be it a panicked exchange while your characters are threatened by imminent danger, or a breathless one, conducted by two lovers during a tryst.

Dialogue that doesn't fulfill at least one (preferably more) of the functions above really has no place in any fiction, of whatever length.

The basics

I'm hoping that most of you know most of this already, but for those who feel rusty or uncertain, here are the rules of the game. (Obviously, if you're Roddy Doyle or Fay Weldon, feel free to skip.)

With very few exceptions, when a new person speaks, you should treat it like a new paragraph i.e. go down to a new line and indent.

'I said I wanted fish fingers for tea,' Julia said. 'Where are they?'
'In the supermarket,' Matt answered. 'Where'd you think?'

However, if a person speaks following a piece of description about them, you can continue with the dialogue on the same line, providing that the description was a new para itself;

Matt wasn't a man who dealt with rejection lightly. 'I'm buggered if I'll let you walk out on me, Julia!'

Note how we know that it's Matt who is speaking. We've remained on the same line, rather than going down a line and indenting, so it's clear the speech is being made by him.

Be careful also to observe all the following the punctuation rules i.e. treat your dialogue as part of your sentence. Take this:

'Julia's rambling on a bit tonight, don't you think, Todd?' said Matt. 'She sure is. I'm fast losing the will to live,' agreed Todd.

Note: 'said' (or 'answered' or 'replied' or 'agreed') is <u>not</u> capitalised, as the dialogue is part of the sentence. Note that it also doesn't matter what precedes it (comma, question mark, exclamation point).

As shown earlier, however, when the speech is a sentence in its own right, the punctuation differs, because now we have two sentences:

'In fact, she's becoming a nine carat bore.' Matt raised a hand to his mouth and stifled a yawn.

Sometimes, however, it helps with the rhythm of your dialogue to attribute your speaker mid sentence. As below:

'Do you think, ' asked Todd, 'that we should ask her to shut up? '

Note how if you do this you treat **the whole thing** as one sentence, as if the attribution wasn't there at all. – In this case, by following 'Todd' with a comma and carrying on. Unless…

'I need to know the time,' said Julia, leaping up from her desk. 'I absolutely have to catch the last train to Cardiff!'

Note that this time, because the attribution happens at the end of a spoken sentence then the next speech starts with a capital letter.

Is all that clear as mud now? I do hope so. And so to some more general bullet points…

Dialogue Dos and Don'ts

Do read your passages of dialogue aloud, to check for rhythm and flow. That sense of rhythm and flow in dialogue can't be taught, it can only be felt. Some call it 'beats', I've heard tell (this is a new thing, I think) and if 'beats' float your boat, see it that way. It should be a feature of all your sentence structure, but it particularly clear in dialogue.

Using **beats** to create **rhy**thm creates a **strange** and pleasing **alch**emy. No, you can't see on the **page** but you can hear it in the **ear**, and it will **make** your work **nic**er to **read**.

Don't overdo it with regional dialects. If you need to make it clear where a character has come from, tread lightly. The odd 'pet' will locate them perfectly clearly in Newcastle, whereas a protracted phonetic outpouring will just grate. Remember, you are not Emily Bronte.

Do make a decision and stick to it re dialogue, particularly if you are setting your action in history or in exotic climes. There's no need to write in a form of special 'olde worlde' English, nor, if your action is wholly set abroad, in 've hav vays of making you talk' type nonsense. If all your characters are Russians, render them in English anyway. Locate them geographically and your readers will be intelligent enough to know that. And if you must have one character with halting broken English, among natives (as I once did), try not to patronise their efforts.

Don't include such a person unless you either a) know one or b) are one. Otherwise, you'll get it wrong and irritate your readers. The same rule applies to teenagers, only more so.

Don't have your characters say what they're doing while they're doing it. One or the other is generally the rule. (As in 'I'll put the kettle on,' she said, putting on the kettle.)

Do prune, and ruthlessly: very few conversations in fiction require either the words 'hello' or 'goodbye'. We can usually kind of take that as read. Similarly…

Don't have a character recount to another character something that just happened to them in the last chapter. 'Oh, my giddy Aunt,' said

Matt, once Julia had told him what had happened… is much the best way to go, almost always.

Do be sparing in your use of screamers!!!!! Though you are allowed a few more in dialogue than in narrative, don't wear out their usefulness by overdoing them. (Unless you work in the genre known as rom-com, that is.)

Conversely, **don't** be afraid to italicise at will in your dialogue. If it were scripted, it would be made clear how an actor should read it, wouldn't it? 'Like *this*, as opposed to like the other, you feckless *mor*on. You went to RADA, you say? Oh, yeah, *sure* you did.'

Do remember to tag information to dialogue discreetly, like vegetables into a faddy child's bolognaise sauce.

Don't worry about having your characters interrupt each other. It adds tension and pace. And lots of white space. Which in turn provides tension and pace…

Attribute indirectly (see the basic rules above). It's not always necessary, or even desirable, to add 'she said' at the end of every utterance. A follow up line such as 'she put her glass down' will make it clear who is speaking.

Finishing a story with a highly charged piece of dialogue often makes for a particularly powerful ending.

Starting a story halfway through a conversation is a good way to draw the reader straight into the action, so don't be afraid to use the technique; you can then flashback to what the conversation began with later.

And finally, **Remember** those useful words 'said' and 'asked' – trust me on this. Mostly, they will do.

Step 5 exercise

Is all about making your dialogue earn its keep as well as looking pretty. Just for fun and brain work (and because we all need to be challenged) see if you can write no more than 500 words, of which almost all is dialogue, which will multitask enough to:

Create Tension: there has been an article in the local rag accusing Matt of affray outside Polly Rocket's Coffee Bar and Pantry in Staines, when Julia thought he was attending a focus group in Ghent. Matt doesn't know she's seen the piece.

Develop the action: We are at the point where Julia is going to confront Matt with her copy of the East Twistleton Gleaner.

Include relevant backstory: Julia makes rag rugs in her spare time, using reclaimed hospital textiles. Matt (who paints) had a nude of Julia in a Royal Academy Summer Exhibition five years ago.

Develop character:

Matt is originally from Dundee, short-tempered, and allergic to milk. Julia used to be a primary school teacher, and always wears hats. Either, but only one, can be your viewpoint character.

Step 6 : Writerly jargon reimagined as geometry…

One of the things that would most vex me when I was an aspiring teenage author was the sense that I wasn't quite 'other' enough. This was partly to do with my father ('what, leave your job in the bank? To do *that*? Are you *mad*? Writing's not a proper job – not for people like us!), and partly due to a misplaced belief that in order to 'be' an author, you needed to be privy to a whole other language – one that couldn't be found within the pages of my Concise OED.

I still have that dictionary, and many words are to be found there; some pleasing, some less so, some absolute gems. Feldspar, for example – how I still long to include the word 'feldspar' somewhere in my fiction. Discombobulate, incubus, wibble.

But, mostly, I was intimidated by jargon. Back then, without the bright clear light of Google there to light the way, I was not a little frightened by much of what passed for sage writerly advice. What on earth did they mean when they referred to a 'character's motivation'? What was a 'protagonist'? Animal, vegetable or mineral? And when people spoke earnestly of the importance of the 'hero's journey', why did I always have a nagging suspicion that they meant something more than what they said?

You, of course, might have all these things accounted for. After all, we *do* have Google – we have the entire internet, and all that's in it. But for anyone who can't define the word 'verisimilitude' at ten paces, here's a quick rundown of what much writerly jargon means over and above it's basic dictionary definition.

Protagonist: This is your hero or heroine. You might have one, one of each, or a trio. Maybe four. Mostly you won't have a lot more than that as a novel is generally based on one or two people's stories.

Adversary/Antagonist: If the protagonist is your 'goodie' then the antagonist is the 'baddie'. Except in novels where the good guy is actually the bad guy but which operates within the parameters of a wholly different society in which morality is defined differently to, well, ours, and.... Forget it. Good sort and bad sort. End of. And this holds true even if, by the end of your story, the bad sort turns out not to be. Clear?

Deus ex machina: As I have already counseled, do look this up. It's a Latin term which essentially means 'don't be lazy and cut corners'. Actually, it doesn't quite, but for the purposes of writing fiction that doesn't matter. Just don't meddle in the natural order of things just to get yourself out of a plot-hole.

Motivation: just as foppish actorly types are apt to bleat 'yes, but what's my motivation?' at weary directors so you should similarly interrogate your characters. Acting in character is all about doing stuff for a reason. You can't have people doing stuff just to get yourself out of a plot-hole. See above.

Melodrama: is where you ham it up (plot twists, character traits and so on) out of all proportion to what's actually happening in your novel, just to get the reader more emotionally engaged. It doesn't work. Readers generally just think 'idiots'. See also : X Factor backstories.

Delayed gratification: you want lots of this. LOTS. The reason people keep reading is because they want to know what happens. The longer you make them wait, the more excited/terrified/fascinated they will be about it, and the more gratitude they will feel when they finally do.

Suspension of disbelief: According to Wikipedia, this term was coined by Samuel Taylor Coleridge, though, sadly, it makes no mention is made of the fact that I met the wife of his great (great?) grandson at an Open University summer school in 1990. Essentially it means injecting enough truth and human interest into your writing that the reader will 'suspend judgment concerning the implausibility of the narrative.' I think we can all get that, can't we?

White space: is the part of the page not marked by letters. In fiction, most agree, a quantity of it is to be desired. It's also a handy by-product of writing dialogue.

Hook: in this context means something that hooks the reader. Think fish. Think of reeling them in with prose so compelling they become putty in your hands.

Cliffhanger: ending your chapters with cliffhangers is one of the surest ways you have of ensuring that your reader will read on. In TV serials, it's the thing that makes people tune into the next episode and in books it's the thing that keeps them up all night till it's done. You want lots of this, too.

Characterisation: seems self-evident, but sometimes isn't. It refers to the depth and breadth of the character you give to – and display in – your human creations. If your characterisation is weak i.e. you haven't created fictional people who feel like real people, then the reader won't care what they get up to.

Conflict: This bears repeating. Without conflict you have no story. Life is a series of often unrelated events. Story, almost always, is a series of related conflicts, which are battled through in order to reach a goal. It's non negotiable.

Verisimilitude: is 'the appearance of being true' – no more, no less. It's what a novel should have in spades, even though it is a falsehood. It's verisimilitude that promotes that suspension of disbelief that STC (further up) was so keen on. Yes, you could just say 'the appearance of being true' but then verisimilitude is a stunningly pretty word, isn't it?

And finally…

Narrative Tension: this is the big one; the jargonista's number one piece of jargon. Narrative Tension is what you achieve by careful observance of – and attention to – all the components described above it. If you maintain a state of tension in your narrative, so the theory goes, you will have created a piece of fiction that people will enjoy reading. Handily, this also tends to work in practice.

But what of geometry? What place does a branch of mathematics have here? Well, none, actually. I include it only because it happens to be part of the name of a chart I once created, in an effort to pull what's written above into a form that could be understood visually. Of course it's nothing to do with geometry. Geometry concerns itself with angles, planes and lines and the complex relationships that exist between them. What I've put together, as anyone can see, is much more 'mind-mappy-flow-charty-web-kind-of-thing'. But as 'writerly jargon re-imagined as 'mind-mappy-flow-charty-web-kind-of-thing'' didn't fit on the page, or indeed sound good, 'geometry' seemed much the better option.

It's old school, this chart, as you can see. Created from paper and ink, using sticky tape and scissors, it's now so dog-eared from use – over so many terms of teaching – that I'm considering laminating the original for posterity. And though I could probably knock up a 21st century version using pixels and some arty app or similar, I'm rather fond of it just as it is.

At the very least, it is, I hope, easy to understand and digest, and shows the relationship to be aimed for between the different ingredients you would hope to incorporate in any given novel. At its centre, naturally, is **narrative tension**, which is achieved (at least in theory) by the three elements around it: **characterisation, conflict and suspense**. Feeding into those are the variables (coloured green) that best support those – from creating worthy adversaries to injecting doses of drama and trauma to that all-important delaying of gratification. (The items in red, I hope you've realized equal things that are To Be Avoided.) The final two elements, written in blue, are **dialogue** and **description,** both with specific roles to play and potential pitfalls.

Not everyone will be able to see a novel in this way, obviously, but if you are fond of popping bracing 'notes to self' above your workplace, you could do worse than consider adding this one to your pile. And that's because understanding the relationship that exists between all these tools and concepts will take you some way down the road of developing the creative intuition that will give your fledgling fiction decent wings.

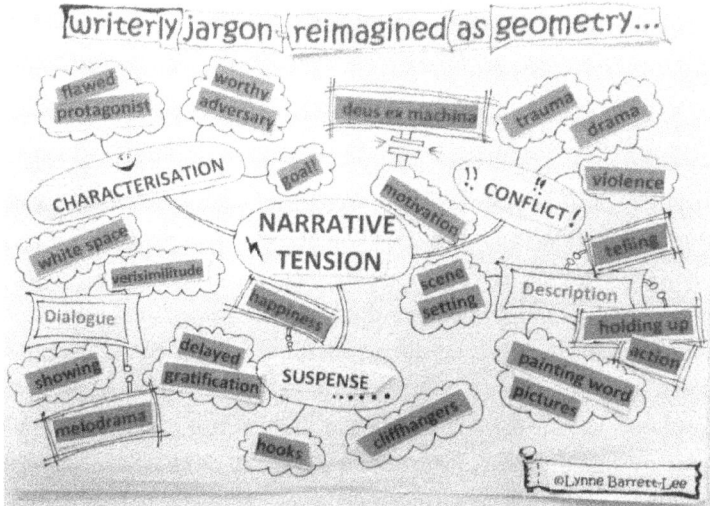

writerly jargon reimagined as geometry...

Step 6 exercise

For those of you who enjoyed the exercise for week 5, this step's task is similar. Take Matt and Julia (they can be a new Matt and Julia, if you like) and write the ending of a watershed chapter for them.... with either: a physical fight between them, an unexpected or highly inappropriate clinch, a crisis befalling both of them at the hands of a third party, or, if you fancy, a murder. Also – just for the mental exercise involved – include the words 'kumquat', 'rotator cuff', 'hole punch' and 'pixelated', in the most imaginative way you can think of, and keeping in mind all the principles discussed above.

Step 7 : Writer's Block

I don't believe in writer's block. There. I've said it. And that's not because I want to pour scorn on those who do; it's just that a) I never had the luxury of being able to afford to and b) one thing I do believe is that if you refuse to believe in something it makes it that much harder for it to impact on your progress.

So what is Writer's Block? Well, to my mind, it's a catch-all expression. The term exists to achieve brevity, and we're all about brevity – and in this case, is a way to scoop up all the reasons why you didn't make any progress today, tie them in a bow, give them a fancy collective name and thus allow you to go and do yoga. Resist its allure! Why you didn't make any progress today can be for all sorts of reasons, which, once you start to analyse them more closely, are far less likely to frighten you into throwing your hands up and screaming 'blocked! I'm so blocked! I feel so *helpless*!'

So let's take a look at them.

If it's because you haven't a clue what you want to write about, then perhaps a career re-think is needed. And no, I'm not being flippant here. If I had a pound for the number of times people have told me, in all seriousness, that they would dearly love to write a novel (the implication usually being that they'd be darned good at it, too) if only they could find something to write about, I would be well on the way to that yacht/Rolex/Caribbean hideaway/insert cliché of your choice.

Never underestimate how much of an element of compulsion is required to be a novelist. If you don't feel compelled to do it, you are unlikely to make it work.

If it's because you know you have a potential novel swirling around in your head, but you are still staring at a blank screen or page, unable to decide what to write in the first place, then you need to type or write 'novel number whatever…' and start writing the first thing that occurs to you. (I find writing 'a novel about a woman who…' is as good a place as any to start. Given time I'd do the maths more comprehensively (even the geometry), but it seems to me that the old equation 'theme + who + what + where + why + how = a story' is a good thing to have scribbled on a post-it nearby. If you know what it is you want to say (adultery sucks, all men/women/Klingons are bastards, there is happiness to be found in sacrifice, etc.) then working out how to say it is simply a question of playing with all the variables (the who, what, where etc.) until you reach a set of them that sets your pulse racing a bit.

Never underestimate the incredible unblocking qualities of just writing the first thing that comes into your head, though. Go on, I dare you. Absolutely no-one needs ever see this.

If your progress has halted even though you've already done that (are ten pages into your slightly hysterical novel-planning type ramblings, perhaps), then you need to print out what you have – trust me, this can work wonders – then sit on the floor with it and highlight all the bits/characters/mad happenings that sound like they might have potential. Cut it up, if you like, portion it out any way that pleases you; the object of the exercise is to jettison what doesn't, gather up the rest, then carry on writing/playing with ideas as before.

Never underestimate the amount of work required to create a whole world and story out of nothing. If it was that easy, everyone would be doing it, wouldn't they? Being disheartened and confounded and stressed at this early stage is entirely appropriate.

If you're stuck because you just wrote a great chapters 1 – 5, but are staring at a page entitled 'Chapter 6' and don't know where to go in the short term, begin by typing the words 'I don't know what I'm doing with this bit yet', plus any of your thoughts, then leave a gap, and get on with writing the next bit you *do* have a handle on – one of those scenes, perhaps, that you wrote a bit of while planning, because you couldn't wait to get them down on paper. Then it's simply a question of bridging a gap between two places, as opposed to jumping off the mothership into a great yawning void.

Never underestimate how draining it is to write a novel. Cling on to any passing piece of flotsam* you can grab. If it's that steamy scene a couple of chapters on, so be it. You are still writing. It's all money in the bank*.

*also allow yourself to mix the odd metaphor. No-one will judge you at this difficult time.

If you're stuck because you don't have any of those scenes in your planning document, then (after slapping your own wrists and breaking a pencil or two) spend a few minutes asking yourself *why* you don't have them, then go straight back to your planning document to put things right. If you can't find any point in your loosely sketched-out novel that excites you enough that you can't wait to write it, then you've still got a bit more work to do on your plot. I really can't emphasise this enough. All the way through the planning bit – at regular intervals during all your mess of 'and then she decides to do this… and then he's in an accident so this happens… and then her mother falls off her kitchen steps and breaks her ankle so she has to go to the hospital just at the point when… and then her boyfriend announces he's been accepted on a mindfulness retreat in Goa…' there should be scenes that you're already itching to write because you can see them so clearly in your head. These are the scenes that, when you come to write them properly, you will initially write without stopping to have him raise an eyebrow, or to look out of the window to see what the weather in your novel is doing that day.

*Never underestimated how complicated it is to create a novel. Expect things like this to happen and find something you **can** write when it does.*

If you're stuck because you're a third of the way through (it's always 30,000 words with me) and it feels as though everything you've written is rubbish, and what's more, you know everything you're going to write subsequently is *also* going to be rubbish, and anyway, even if you do manage to finish it, you won't be able to find an agent for it, and even if you get one, he/she won't be able to find a publisher for it because *everyone* knows it's virtually impossible to get anything published these days unless you've been on Love Island or had implants the size of pumpkins, so what's the point in bothering in the first place, etc., etc., then join the club. Because it's right here that many, many, many novels flounder, and many novelists-in-waiting, sadly, give up. So at this point you have three choices. Either you keep writing (by far the best bet), start writing something better (if you really must – starting afresh can get very addictive), or you put what you've done in that ubiquitous drawer till your writer's block sorts itself out (NO!).

Never underestimate how easy it is to talk yourself into giving up at this point. You and thousands of others. Make a pact with yourself to finish. Even if you think it's rubbish you have at least finished a novel. The value of knowing that is immense.

Finally, if you have writer's block because you *did* finish a novel and all of the above *did* happen, and STILL, all this time later, you're not anywhere near being published (and you can't afford surgery or the post traumatic stress of having humiliated yourself on reality TV) then the same still applies. You either go back to writing or you give up on writing. Ouch. That sounds horrible. But it's all you can do.

Never underestimate that novel writing is HARD. No, not 'down a mine' hard, not 'emergency, life-saving surgery' hard. But it's not like going into an office every day. There is no pay (at this stage), no deadline (at this stage), no professional kudos or respect (at this stage) and no support network of colleagues physically on hand (at any stage). All you have to support you are desire and ambition, bloodymindedness and doggedness; all qualities that can desert you, and often do.

Let's be clear. Repeated episodes of struggling to make progress are normal. They are not 'blocks' so much as logical reasons why you struggle to move forwards from time to time. However, if they are such a feature of your writing life that you are floundering in the long term, then perhaps your Writer's Block (if we must) is just nature's way of limbering you up slowly for making the decision that you don't much enjoy writing fiction after all. So, if you're serious about your writing, don't **let it creep up on you while you're not looking**. Don't let it become a habit. Almost everyone I know who is currently successful is essentially not there just because they got lucky. It's because they wrote more, and more *often*, than similarly talented writers, so their chances of getting lucky we're hugely increased. It's just the same as it is with short fiction. If you write and send out a new story a week, you have much more chance of success than someone who only sends out one every two months.

Can you see a pattern here? Or, better still, a theme? Okay, then, if we must. A truism. That the only way to get a novel written is to write.

The Muse

To be honest, I'm only adding this bit because it gives me another chance to bang on about a favourite bug bear of mine, but it probably bears banging on about anyway. The fact is that the only way to guarantee that inspiration will strike joyously and often is to make a point of *always* writing, whether it's present or not. The more you write, the more assured you get at it. I didn't used to believe that, but it really is true. Which is not to say that there is some sort of 'literary greatness continuum', upon which all published authors are still travelling as they go about their work. If that were so then all first novels would be rubbish and all last novels masterpieces (often the reverse is true). It's just that if you want to write for a living and not as a sideline, then it's sensible to adopt that pavement artist mentality. Once you get the hang of it, you relax a tiny bit, because you know you can do it again. And once you know you can do it again, you spend a lot less time agonising over the agonising and accept it as part of the process of creation. Which leaves you all freed up to get on with your writing.

Step 7 exercise

At this stage, I'm all for a little navel gazing. In my face-to-face course, this is the point where I ask my students – now armed with a small bag of tricks and a long list of 'must do's – to reflect on their writing ambitions. Only, on this occasion, with a twist. Pen a few hundred words – more if you like – about who you are and, in writing terms, what it is you dream of. Don't be bashful; unless you're a compulsive blogger, nobody but you ever needs to see it.

One proviso. Write it in third person, as if looking down at yourself, huddled at your keyboard or kitchen table or favourite bench in the park, as if you were a character in your own novel.

Step 8 : The Hard Part

(The art of being a jobbing writer)

I thought long and hard about what to call this step in the process. After all, we have already covered most of the bases; looked at planning and plotting, research and first pages, characterisation, motivation, dialogue and sub plots. We've mulled over viewpoint and timescales and tenses, and most recently we've touched on the idea of writer's block.

So what next? What goes next on our novel writing checklist? What sits between 'this is how you construct your magnum opus' and 'here's a few tips to make someone sit up and take notice'? (That someone, by the way, being someone in a position to put your great work into the hands of a reader – not a reader themselves; a completely different task.)

It finally struck me that only one title was apposite, because once you're at this stage, you really are on your own. Yes, you can elicit feedback from fellow writers, attend classes, join circles, read books like this one (you could even dabble in online 'novel writing formulas' if you must – though please don't) but the truth is that tens of thousands of words need to be written and no-one can do that but you. And that is, without question, the hard part.

It's hard work for a professional writer who has no other demands on their time or mental energy (not to mention a publishing deal and an editor eager to get their hands on it), so do not underestimate the demands it will place on poor lonely you, the unpublished and anxious.

In her excellent book, *Bestseller*, the author Celia Brayfield lists the most common difficulties that beset the would-be novelist as the 'ten trials'. These are: the telephone (don't answer it), significant others (deflect their attentions), children (temporarily ignore them), strangers (don't answer the door to them), animals (place them out of earshot), housework (don't do it), errands (send someone else), personal commitments (postpone them) hunger (resist), and, finally, sleep (drink lots of coffee).

Note, Celia doesn't mention social media, but that's only because she wrote the book before it existed. In the 21st century, it would be numero uno. Be very afraid of the siren call of social media.

If any of these irritants tend to interfere with your progress then it obviously makes sense to address them. Before facebook and twitter my personal *bête noire* always used to be my mother, who lived far away and used to come to stay for a week at a stretch. If this ever coincided with an intense writing phase (it did often, of course, as it's my job) then I could readily be whipped into a murderous fury, just by the sound of her heels clicking resentfully around the place, and her endlessly popping her head round the door to enquire if I'd like a cup of tea. Had I an office job, this would never have happened. I'd have simply left her at home with my ironing pile. Had I *any* sort of 'job' job this would never have happened either. My sister runs a science laboratory in California, for example, and my mum would think twice about even *emailing* her, such would be her fear of 'being a nuisance', let alone daring to call and attempting to talk to her.

You must expect this sort of misunderstanding about the nature of what you're doing and whether it counts as 'proper work'. There is nothing you can do about living in a society that treats people who toil for nothing as 'not properly working'. Nothing to be done about people who think, since you're home, that you're not working half as hard as Bob down the road, who gets a bus or train to his place of work. Nothing to be done about that quiet lack of support, because what you're doing is, well, let's be honest, if you believe them, a bit unrealistic. So what should you do? Well, it's simple. The biggest trick, while gently batting away those who seek to interrupt you, is to resist the temptation to agree with them **on any level**. And you'll be tempted. Yes you will. At some point, you will become an apologist for your own ambitions. But if you do that, you will give up, guaranteed.

Far more important than any of the devices mentioned above, then, is that you approach writing a novel with the same degree of commitment that you would any other form of employment. Fanciful and charming though it might seem to talk loftily in terms of muses and moments of inspiration and other flim-flam (and comforting though it is to hear of Great Novels that were years in the making) the reality is that if you are lucky enough to be published in the first place, your editor may well expect novel number 2 to be on their desk within a year.

I think it was Phillip Pullman who pointed out that 12 months is not a lot, given that your first novel took you *your whole lifetime*. Remember, it wasn't just the period of writing that counted but the whole lifetime's worth of amassed Great Wisdoms, turns of phrase, pithy or amusing anecdotes, character studies, storylines and brilliant ideas. It stands to reason, then, that it's immeasurably helpful to add commitment, self-discipline and dogged self-belief to the talent, imagination and facility for language that you have already demonstrated you have.

In her 1995 book, *Writers on Writing*, Alison Gibbs spoke to a number of commercially successful fiction writers, and Jeffrey Archer related something that I felt summed this up perfectly. He'd been approached by a surgeon acquaintance who'd written a novel and was keen to elicit some feedback. As the book details, this was it:

> *'Archer's written response, having read it, was this:*
> *'Did you write this between doing operations?'*
> *The surgeon rang him up and said, 'yes. How did you know?'*
> *'Well,' Archer replied, 'There are some good chapters, bad chapters, middling chapters…how insulting!'*
> *'What do you mean by that?' asked the stunned surgeon.*
> *'I mean that it's totally insulting,' went on Archer. 'How would you feel if I told you that I was about to start doing operations*

between writing chapters? You'd be insulted [I think I'd also be a tad
anxious – LBL]. And I'm insulted by you writing chapters between
surgeries – now go away!"

In short, I think that what he was trying to say was don't short change your reader by offering up second rate work. The surgeon did apparently take the advice on board and went on to work harder on, and also publish, his book. And the advice – whatever your thoughts about Jeffrey Archer – is sound. In order to write a decent novel you've got to commit a decent amount of time, effort and professionalism to the task; treat both it, and your desire to be published, with respect. This is often less straightforward than it sounds, not only for the practical reasons to which Celia Brayfield alludes, but also for reasons of self-consciousness and feeling a lack of entitlement – who are you to suppose you might become a novelist? What breathtaking arrogance!

While you can't deal with those feelings by simply ticking boxes or telling yourself otherwise, getting mentally focussed and treating the task as a job will go a long way to counteract them. If you persist in treating writing as a hobby you fit in around other things (work and family commitments, having a good time, whatever) then that's the place it will always have in your life. And, yes, it might get you one novel written.... eventually. But for every one published novel that nets its author a fortune, there are tens of thousands that earn next to nothing for their creators. Again, if that's all you want, fine. But if your dream is to one day make your writing your day job, then you have to find regular space and time to write; not just as the fancy takes you, but when it *doesn't* take you too.

Jeffrey Archer has also been quoted as saying that it's impossible, in his judgement, to do another job at the same time as writing a novel. His advice would be to plan five or six weeks when you can take yourself off and just do it. At first glance, this might seem an impossible dream, (bar, er, pandemics) but if you have spent several months planning your novel to the nth degree, as many writers (myself included) do, then this isn't outside the bounds of possibility – and don't forget, the planning stage is one that *can* slot in around other commitments – benefit from them, even.

If that idea daunts you, however, then you must find a regular space in your diary and commit it to your writing – ideally at a time you've identified as being one when you feel particularly creative. Yes, it takes discipline to make yourself get up at 5 am every morning, or work long into the night, but if that's what you have to do, then that's what you *must* do. The more erratic your mental prioritisation of your novel, the harder it will be to focus when you do write, and the writing will suffer as a consequence. Just as with reading, if you only pick up the story sporadically, and have to try and recall all that went before it, then your interest in and connection to the story will flag. Ideally, by the actual writing stage, it will be the first thing you think about when you wake up in the morning and the last thing in your head when you go to bed at night.

And, obviously, at all points in between.

Step 8 exercise

Here's a *who where when what why* for you to get your teeth into:

Alexander
The Museum of Modern Art in New York
December 1999
A poisoning
A lie

Give yourself no more than half an hour and see what you can do with those in a page of writing.

Step 9 : Recipes for Success

There is, of necessity, a bit of a mental pause here. It's at this point in the process (when I'm teaching my course, certainly) where I feel I've said all I can say about how to write a novel and must leave you to do the business of actually making one. Yes, if I were your personal mentor, we might get together on a regular basis, to chew over the odd scene, the odd glitch, the odd crisis of confidence, but of course I'm not, so you're mostly on your own.

As I was. When I wrote my first novel (actually, hang on, my every novel, and narrative non-fiction book, ever since) I worked entirely in isolation, partly because that's the nature of the job and partly, I'll admit, because I didn't want anyone seeing it – not till I was done, at least. You might feel differently – you might wish to elicit feedback at every stage, but I'm going to stick my neck out (and remember, this is just one opinion) and suggest you try and resist the urge to 'share' during the creative process, as what matters more than anything is that this is your creative vision; and, as with most things creative, I find, too many cooks can so easily spoil the broth. Think about art – is it normal for a painter to involve others? Hand over the brush, pass over the palette, and invite a friend to step up to the easel and contribute a few daubs? You may disagree, of course, but at least give it some thought. It's easy to end up, as an editor friend experienced in such matters once observed, with a book that reads like its been written by a committee.

So. Back to you, and the hard task ahead, and the need to get tens of thousands of words down on paper or screen, while taking in all the jargon previously mentioned. In writing utopia, of course, all these buzzwords wouldn't even feature; creating your novel in such a way that you achieve that narrative tension would be an organic process from the outset, informed by years of reading and unconsciously absorbing all the rules. In writing utopia the only people who would analyse the storytelling process would be academics wishing to deconstruct the nuts and bolts of it, and the critics who wish to rip it all apart.

Sadly, most of us don't live in utopia, and for most of us, the process of writing full length fiction tends to need a touch more thought and application in order for the organic bit to actually begin happening. For every genius who just writes without thinking and gets published-to-great-acclaim, there are thousands more (and, yes, I know this is my constant moan) with drawers full of unfinished, muddled, stalled novels or – worse, to my mind, because of the sheer depressing size of them – finished ones that are simply not quite good enough.

It's a sad reality that in some drawers, here and there, there will also be gems; novels bristling with life and competence and readability, which have simply fetched up in the wrong place at the wrong time. But the brutal truth is that if you've cast your net wide with your precious manuscript and have still failed to attract the attention of a single agent, then it's probably time to take a long hard look at the thing and see if you can identify where you've gone, or are going, wrong.

Bear one thing in mind at all times. That writing a novel is (sorry to repeat myself) hard work. Just as there is a huge chunk of slog between a young athlete forming a grand ambition and going on to win an Olympic medal, so there is a serious amount of hard work between the thrill of initial creation (oh, that stunning idea! That magnificent first chapter!) and the glittering prize of being able to write 'The End'. The actual writing bit – the point where you manoeuvre your characters, plot and setting into position and begin to play the thing out, will make huge demands on your technical abilities as a storyteller; what to put where, how to pay out your storyline, what to focus in on, which threads to weave where.

65

So, just as it makes sense to analyse while you're writing it, it also makes sense to put it away for a bit, then return *to it and read it again*. And do it ruthlessly. Not in the sense of constant nit-picking and fussing, but by reviewing the big picture and asking yourself if what you've done is likely to tick all the boxes we discussed earlier on in this course. In this way, with luck and talent and application, you might just avoid the sort of problems that agents and publishers, when rejecting you, routinely cite. Such as...

'It just didn't grip me enough...'

If you keep finding yourself plunging into troughs of lassitude when you re-read your novel, then you can be sure your reader will too. The aim for all writers is to get a reader so hooked on their story that putting the book down becomes a real struggle. There is no magic bullet to help you achieve this. Neither is it something that happens by itself. If there's one thing you must keep in mind at all times it is that you must strive to create that magic state of **narrative tension**, and so, by extension, tension in your reader. This applies to every genre of novel and consists of two simple things we've already discussed: a) that they care about the characters you've created, and b) that those characters are involved in some sort of struggle, rather than gambolling merrily through life. As soon as you stop jerking on their strings in this way, the desire to read on will slip away. Thus you must think like an emotional puppet master: set up a constant round of crises and traumas and make the reader wait for you to sort them.

'Something about the character/s just didn't ring true...'

If this criticism is levelled at your work, then you probably have a problem with **motivation**. Remember that one? To speak of your character's 'motivation' isn't the pretentious drama school twaddle it might sound, but the serious business of ensuring that your characters behave properly *in* character at all times. This means reacting to their various crises and traumas in a believable and recognisable way *for them*. If they over-react to some minor blip, for example, because your plot demands they do, you create the dreaded **melodrama**, which agents and readers alike hate. Similarly, if their personality is so off the wall that their actions are mostly unguessable, no-one normal will much empathise with them. Which is not to say characters should be stereotypical, but that they must employ universal human emotions. (Unless they are Martians, of course.) The best way to deal with motivational problems is to know your characters' backstories really well; we are all the sum total of our previous experience, after all.

'There's some good writing here, but it just felt a bit flat in places…'

Sorry to repeat myself on the subject of **conflict**, but if you're getting bogged down, start a fight. It's amazing the number of amateur novels that fail to employ this simple trick. They sometimes read almost as if the writer, like that characters, is emotionally or physically knackered from time to time, and needs the odd period to lie around and rest up. No! Watch an episode of any soap or other TV drama, and you'll see that characters are *at all times* engaged in conflict situations, and you must strive to achieve this as well. Not because your aim is necessarily to write a novel-like-a-soap-opera, but simply because drama is conflict and conflict is drama. Thus the only time you should give your characters' a break, is when you're setting them up for something even worse to happen. This is true of all novels till the very last chapter, and, ideally, the very last paragraph.

'It just seemed to lose its way…'

Given the technical demands that I've already mentioned are going to be placed on you once your novel is up and running, it won't come as much of a surprise if I tell you that you're likely to encounter some pot holes along the way. The best pre-plotting in the world is not infallible; make some small change to either the action or the characters and you will soon observe the Butterfly Effect in action. At the writing stage, an easy remedy is to bend it very slightly out of shape to accommodate whatever it is you've found vital to tinker with. But do not! Few things are more glaring than one of those pesky ***deus ex machina*** interventions by an author – where, as we have learned by now (I hope) something completely unexpected happens just to repair a plot inconsistency. Trust me, when you return to it, it will jar, even for you, who created it. The only sure way to sort out plot headaches is to go back and re-organise your plot. This may – probably will – mean a big stint of rewriting, but remember – your book has to be as good as it can be. There'll always be the next one on the pile waiting to be read.

Hmm. Am I repeating myself here? Good.

Stories and storytellers who got it right

Everyone has their own shortlist of novels that imply wowed them – rocked their world, floated their boat, knocked their socks off, blew them away – and no two people's are ever going to be the same. That's as it should be, and we should celebrate that kind of diversity of thought and feeling, but, since we're talking about recipes for success what we should also do is look at the things they had in common. Consider this:

'What should you write? There are very few rules and some of those that do exist will often be broken – sometimes disastrously, sometimes triumphantly. But you need to start with the raw DNA of story-telling. What does every successful novel have in common, in some form, however mutant? The obvious elements are a gripping story; imaginative and distinctive writing; and enthralling characters. The story doesn't need to be heavy with plot, but it does have to hook from the first paragraph and keep you turning the pages. The writing doesn't have to emulate a literary giant, but it does need to have its own appropriate, attractive voice, avoiding verbal cliché at

all costs. The characters need not be loveable or even likeable, but they must be people with whom you are very happy to spend time; strong, memorable and human.'

David Smith – The Handbook of Creative Writing

It doesn't do to be so down on yourself that you feel constantly tempted to give up on both your novel and all hope, but once you've reached the point of no going back – wherever that may be – begin to be rigorously self-critical about the novel *you* are writing, making reference to those 'must haves' above. Do not ignore any voice in your head that says 'that doesn't sound right/feel right/ seem right. Plot, character, motivation or twist – if any aspect of what you're doing isn't working, change it; remember, while lots of us don't know why the books we love work, we can usually see instantly why they don't.

Books we love – and that sell widely through word of mouth (generally the best way) – usually have all of the above. But something else as well – some sort of quirk, unique aspect, deep resonance or plain old wow factor, that lift them from the crowd. It's worth trying to tease out what that might consist of in your own work. Here's a list – chosen off the top of my head, after a quick glance at one of my bookshelves, at random – of books that, it seemed to me, when I read them, to have that. Be they genre defining or gender defying, not for nothing have they done so well, in so many ways:

Hi Fidelity by Nick Hornby: written by a man, but with a very female focus on confession and emotion. This was groundbreaking at the time – blokes had feelings. Oh my!

Bridget Jones' Diary by Helen Fielding – was all about the likeability and pathos of the character. Diary-style books had been done many times before, but Fielding's creation was so fresh, so sweet, and so utterly adorable that she was impossible for men and women not to love.

The Road Home by Rose Tremain – inhabiting the heart and mind of an eastern European immigrant was a master stroke – this was published at a time when Eastern European migrants had just begun arriving in the UK and there was an air of anxious change in the air. Here, too, was a character our society was, at that time, subtly telling us to distrust, or feel threatened by. Seeing *our* society through *his* eyes was riveting and thought-provoking.

The Horse Whisperer by Nicholas Evans; never underestimate the strength of a dramatic, sweeping and beautiful canvas on which to play out your human story. This also had one of the most gripping first chapters I've ever read. The story, from then on, never sagged.

One Shot by Lee Child – Jack Reacher is the archetypal hero for this kind of narrative – a man every male reader wants to be and every female reader wants to seduce. Very strong sense of right, wrong and (rough) justice. Lee Child had a real winner up his sleeve with his avenging angel too – the staggeringly original device of Jack being a man who *owns nothing*.

Saturday by Ian McEwan – set over one 24 hour period, in one place (the Saturday of the anti-war protests in central London in the late 1990s) this was a master class in structure. It was also a master class in the skill of showing how one single event can so dramatically shape and alter a life.

The Road by Cormac McCarthy – McCarthy's writing style is so singular you might struggle for a page or six, thinking 'can he *really* do that and get away with it?' Yes he can. Bleak and oh-so beautiful, this post-a-nameless-apocalypse novel was, for me, unputdownable.

Room by Emma Donoghue – another 'right place right time' winner, certainly, but this was a book that would hit home at any time. Told from the perspective of a five year old child, this stand-out book is so singular that any attempt to describe it would be pointless. More to the point, it would also be an unforgiveable spoiler. And I wouldn't be so mean to you. Just go and read it.

The Signature of All Things by Elizabeth Gilbert – astonishing, imaginative, and totally unique – quite simply like nothing else I have ever read. Probably the book I most wish I'd written.

Everyone has their own collection of must-read books; the trick is to make *your* book good enough – unique enough – to end up in several someone else's lists. Be tough on yourself, therefore. If any part feels flat, or flaccid, or too 'tell instead of show', then go back and think of ways to make it better. You're aiming to reach that 'unputdownable' quality that will lift your own novel from the masses.

In short, re-write, re-write, re-write – keep going till your work is as perfect as it can be. Remember, masterful works rarely flow, fully formed, from writers' pens; a huge part of writing skill – the craft – is in the re-writing. To misquote a famous quote 'the hardest writing results in the easiest reading'. If it's easy on the reader's eye, it's likely to have been the result of an awful lot of tweaking and twiddling. So, no matter how desperate you are to get your creation out in public, at no point be tempted to skip this step. This is because in order to connect with a real reader, you first have to impress both an agent and a publisher, which complicates the matter no end. Consider this comment from a reader who posted on an online forum, musing on the differences between what a reader wants and what a publisher wants;

'All comes down to money I expect! How many books have been written that a reader would enjoy if only the book had the chance to be published? Full lists, changing markets, cuts in budgets all must

make a difference to how many books/authors are taken on. From everything I've read, agents/publishers want polished books from authors that have a long shelf life (as in long term writing rather than books left on the bookshop shelves unsold!). There are so many submissions per day that your book has to grip from paragraph one. An original angle, an interesting story line, strong believable characters all matter. If publishers/agents are going to invest time and money into an author, they want to know that they are going to get more than one book and that they don't have to wait 5 years for it.'

In short, you must set your standards almost impossibly high. And prepare to do battle.

Step 9 exercise

Time to step away from the keyboard. The most important thing you can do for your novel now is to put it away somewhere and ignore it. Ignore it completely for a month, perhaps. Two. Even three. In an ideal world, at any rate, because it will put space between the two of you, and that space is what will enable you to see it more clearly when next you cast a gimlet eye upon it.

In reality, of course, this might prove difficult. I finished my first novel and had printed it and sent it to an agent within 24 hours of its completion. But there is a strong case for doing as I say here, rather than as I did, because experience has shown me that it really makes a difference when you look at what you've written with a fresh eye.

So be strong, put that mental pen down, and do something else instead, like making jam, wallpapering the spare room, walking the dog, walking the neighbour's dog, or maybe sketching out a loose plan for bringing about world peace. Do anything you like. Just don't you dare touch that novel.

Step 10: Blurbs revisited

(and synopses wrestled into shape)

The previous step notwithstanding (it was there just to make a point, really) there is *some* useful writing you can do. In fact, there are several writing-related things that you should be doing while your novel is fermenting. They are, in no particular order of priority:

Writing a blurb

Writing a synopsis

Researching agents

Writing your next novel/the outline for your next novel/any ideas you already have that might form the basis of your next novel/the words 'help – I can't think what to write about for my next novel (delete as appropriate).

Clearing your desk and your mind of the world of your first novel and labelling a file, both in (virtual) reality and in your head, with the words 'Novel no. 1', followed by the title.

If time permits, reacquainting yourself with your human

family. (This last step is optional but there is much to recommend it.)

Blurbs – some thoughts

As previously noted, it's not that difficult to get the gist of what a blurb (or to define it properly: 'descriptive or commendatory matter.') is. There is one on pretty much every fiction (and non-fiction) book you've ever read. In a hardback it's to be found inside the front jacket flap, and in a paperback, you'll find it on the back.

Length. How long should a blurb be? Between 100 and 200 words is the norm for a paperback. Most first novels are published as paperbacks.

Punctuation. A blurb has its own conventions in this regard. This is the one time when hyperbole is all – really, it SO is!!! – which means a general amnesty on exclamations marks, ellipses and multiple question marks.

Blurbs need hooks. Pose many questions and **on no account** answer them.

Include superlatives – used judiciously, they will out. But at the same time, beware – do not use incontinently, or they will be rendered invisible.

You are officially allowed to insert any word you like into the following 'by an author of ….. talent', 'a novel of …... , ……. and …….' and 'A story which encompasses ….. and …. and is told with ……. and great ……..'

(The word 'utterly', in this context is probably non-negotiable, and can be slipped in front of any superlative employed, as above.)

The more famous you are the less blurb you need, as it takes up space that can be filled with impressive reviews and more superlatives – this time about you. The word 'master' in this context is essential.

Writing a blurb is, as I hope you've gathered from above, the fun part. And now you have a novel under your belt, a bit of welcome light relief; now's the time when you can hone your early foray into creating 'puff' for your fledgling work into something sharp and focused; something an editor might be grateful have appear on their desk to spare them having to do it for you. It also shows you have a handle on where your book lies in the grand scheme of things. What sort of 'flavour' it has, what 'intention', what 'tone' it intends to set.

Writing a blurb, in the scheme of things, is easy. As are many things (quantum mechanics, perhaps, understanding Fermat's last theorem, chess) when compared to that *other* thing, called 'writing a synopsis'. In short, brace yourself. The fun stops right here.

'But why do you even need a synopsis?' I hear you cry. You've written the book now, haven't you? Why can't they just read it? Well, the truth is that, by and large, they can't be bothered. (By, 'they', I refer of course to literary agents. People who, at the time of writing, at least, still provide by far the most popular and certain route into mainstream publication, which, despite the whole ebook self-publishing revolution – more of which later – is the kind most budding authors most want.)

This is not unreasonable. If your inbox is bombarded by unsolicited manuscripts on a daily basis then it makes sense to do anything to minimize the time spent in sifting through the unpublishable to find the gems. A synopsis provides one way to do this. Read in conjunction with your (excellent, astonishing, compelling etc.) opening chapters, it gives a clue as to whether your brilliance, already noted, is accompanied by a half-decent plot.

But enough of the whys and wherefores – we'll return to them later. For now all you need to know is that you *do* need a synopsis, and that there's no time like the present, given that you've now *written your entire novel*, to sit down and get on and write it.

The dreaded synopsis….some pointers

Most agents and small publishers (big ones rarely, if ever, accept unsolicited work) are kind enough to state what they're after. In most cases a page or two of synopsis (A4, 12 point font, single spaced) is what's required. If you're super-driven, and slightly masochistic, therefore, creating one of each length might be an idea.

Always write in present tense, even if your novel is written in past tense. Present tense will give it forward momentum, as if the reader is watching the action unfold.

Start as you mean to go on – impressively. That first couple of sentences must really grip, so think hard about them. Hook the reader's attention from the off. You might want to begin your synopsis with either your blurb, or a snippet from an early scene.

Consult your outline. Go back to that point in your original planning, where you identified those key stepping stones that took you from start to finish. They will form the skeleton of your synopsis.

Remember, your synopsis should be all about your MAIN plot. There's no need to wander off to explain the details of your subplots. The editor/agent will assume they will be there. Unless one of them is integral to making sense of the denouement, only mention briefly, if at all.

Keep the synopsis active. Have people make things happen as opposed to things happening TO them. Make sure your protagonist/s is/are seen to drive the story.

Make your synopsis read with as much narrative pull as your manuscript. It's not a blurb – full of puff – but neither is it a list of ingredients. Think SHOW and not TELL as you write.

DON'T try to 'sell' your story to the reader. That's strictly for the blurb. Avoid the urge to come over all 'voiceover' man. Strike out anything that smacks have being the linguistic equivalent of a drum roll; taglines such as 'is her destiny written in the stars?' or 'can one day change your life?' These are devices for the jacket-designing stage.

Do include snippets of particularly punchy dialogue. While you're not describing scenes here, you still need some sense of the characters coming to life, and a sprinkling of pithy one-liners will brighten up the page.

Don't use block punctuation. (This book is written is block punctuation.) Lay out your synopsis as you would your novel. Similarly, don't right hand justify – leave that edge raggedy. Yes, novels ARE right justified, but they contain lots of dialogue, which creates white space, which signals story, which creates that oh-so-desirable 'ooh, what's going to happen next?' thing.

Edit it, then go away, then come back, then edit again. If you have experience of personal-statement writing for UCAS (or other University application device), think similarly. Make every line as perfect as it can be.

Trawl for passive sentences that don't move things forward. Don't waste precious word count by interrogating your story: will everything be okay? Is this going to change everything? Is he the man for her? Etc., etc.

If you can shoehorn in the reason for/relevance of your book's title, do. It will make the editor/agent go 'ahhh…' which is good.

Include the ending. This is not a tease – it's a professional pitch.

If you have an idea for writing a sparkling synopsis that ignores half of the above, then trust your instincts and go for it. That's what I did.*

*Born more out of desperation than any bolt of creative lightening striking me, the synopsis for my first novel was rather different to what's above in some ways, as it took the form of a letter from my heroine, Julia, addressed to me. 'Dear Lynne,' it began, 'how are you? Long time no speak! God, you won't BELIEVE all the things that have happened to me these past few months, you really won't. You know Richard cheated on me, right? Yes, of <u>course</u> you do – I remember Carol telling me she'd told you. Well, as you know, I kicked him out – you'd have done the same, I'm sure – I was LIVID. Well….' I then proceeded to relate, in similar breathy chatty manner, the plot of the novel with became *Julia Gets a Life*. I have no way of knowing whether it influenced my agent more than it might have had I done it differently – and never will. What I do know – and I'd urge you to approach things with a similar mindset – was that as soon as I started writing it that way, it just *felt* right. And I polished it off in no time, thus allowing me to ignore the sage advice given here earlier, and get it out in the post that very day.

Step 10 exercise

Is obvious, I hope. One blurb, one synopsis, one neatly labelled file. Tea and cake with loved ones. That's an order.

Step 11 – Editing

First up, a definite. You will do a much better job of editing if you stick rigidly to two rules:

One is that you leave it for as long as you can stand: a month is a good minimum, if you can bear it. Longer is even better. Trust me on this. Because it's true. Also note that it's the reason you've found my notes on editing here, rather than earlier, because, as with a joint of beef, you'll find the process much smoother if you leave your creation to rest.

Two is that you are ruthlessly perfectionist in your approach. After months (perhaps years) of having to big yourself up mentally just to find the courage to do this, now you must turn traitor on yourself. Remind yourself at all times that you are not as good as you think you are. Because, honestly, you're not. And neither am I. If you observe rule one, you have a much better chance of seeing this.

Remember, there are two distinct types of editing. **Macro** (this isn't some official language, by the way – it's just how I see it) in which you see major changes that will need making to the plot and structure, and **Micro**, where you pay attention to the writing style, sentence by sentence. When your book lands at a publishing house, they will do both of these again, only they will call them a structural edit and a line edit.

Macro Editing

As with the rules above, there are two types of novelist. There's the first kind, who throw the switch on their inner editor, then write like fury, terrified that if they don't, they'll lose momentum. In order to achieve them, they keep up a motivational patter along the lines of 'hell, it'll all come out right in the end: I'll just keep going – I can sort any chaos I've created later'. Novelists of this kind have a BIG Macro task ahead. And the moral of the story is: **TRY NOT TO BE LIKE THIS**. If you plan your novel properly, and know the outline so well you could sit down and recite the whole of it from memory, there's a good chance you won't have to do any Macro editing, because any inconsistencies will already have made their presence known, and you'll have corrected them before you started writing them.

I CANNOT EMPHASISE ENOUGH HOW INVALUABLE IT IS TO HAVE A STONKING GREAT TEN THOUSAND WORD OUTLINE.

So, editing should be part of what you do *while* you're writing. Not in the sense that you keep holding yourself up and losing flow, but in that if something feels like it's not working out, you always **stop**. And then **think**. And **sort it out** before moving on. Of course, if you haven't already done this then two things will happen. Either your talent has prevailed and it's all hanging together anyway – in which case, your Macro edit should be straightforward – or you realise that the little niggle you felt when you were writing it was correct, and you need to make major structural changes. There is no tick list that will magically sort this process out for you, I promise. As with knitting, you'll need to go back to where the problem happened, work out why, how it can be remedied, and just do it. It will be a very big, very dispiriting job.

IT WILL ALSO REMIND YOU HOW TRULY INVALUABLE IT IS TO HAVE A STONKING GREAT TEN THOUSAND WORD OUTLINE.

Obviously, even with a comprehensive outline in place, it might be that your novel writing skills still need work, which means that, even having followed yours, the book you've ended up with doesn't hang together as well as you would like. Again, there is no tick list that will sort this out for you. It's something *you* need to feel/see/absorb via osmosis. If you can't see what's wrong with it, it's going to be almost impossible for you to fix it, which means the only advice I can give in that regard is to trust any tiny voice, EVER, that whispers 'this isn't working', however depressing it is to contemplate the amount of work required to fix it. Remember, that voice never lies. The one that does lie is the one that says 'this is good *enough*'. And if you listen to it, yours will most likely be one of those manuscripts that agents return, sighing, thinking, 'hmm, some good stuff here, but this novelist's not quite there yet. Next!'

Micro Editing

Ah. This is always so much easier. When micro editing your novel, some points to consider…

Editing is not necessarily about removal. When I edit my novels, they invariably end up longer. This is because I'm a dialogue-loving writer, and dialogue (if pacy) tends to give novels pace. So there's generally room to slip in extra detail. The first editor's note for my first ever published novel was this, on around page 40: 'Lynne, I'm getting a great sense of what Richard's *like*, but what does he actually LOOK like? I have no idea'. So wrapped up in my heroine's voice was I (hell, she was married to him, so she already *knew* what he looked like) that I had entirely neglected to describe him physically. Which is not to say chapter and verse was required – it rarely is – but just slipping in a line about his 'charcoal-eyed, pillar of the community features' did the trick.

Editing *is* more often about removal than addition. In the full flow of creativity writers are apt to get over-excited about 'saying stuff'. But remember, less is generally more. And if you're a good editor you'll know that losing that 'generally' gives that sentence more clout.

Remove excess qualifiers such as really, very, extremely and so on. Trust me, most writers have a few too many. Strike out 'quite' with the zeal of, well, a zealot.

Check for 'adjectival groups of three'. You are not Barbara Cartland. Any character you have saddled with the misfortune to have been born with long dark flowing hair, big blue limpid eyes, a warm, generous, full-lipped smile and a warm, sunny, positive approach to life deserves to be re-located to a better book than yours.

Check for adjectival groups of two, as well. And remove any that come as a two-for-one offer in your brain. That full heaving bosom, those black button eyes, that brown leather handbag, that fluffy white cloud, that little old lady, those grumpy old men…

Think Sacher! And then 'torte', and then 'tautology'. The expression 'great big' has no place in fiction. Neither does 'tiny little' or 'most perfect'.

Look out for tics. Mine are 'basically, 'clearly' and 'of course' (as you might have noticed). I also have people nod a lot. Oh, and a tendency to overuse – or so I'm told, anyway – the device of the mid-sentence dash.

Tread lightly when dealing with your characters' emotions. In the heat of creation you might have them tending towards melodrama: How could he do this to me? How? How could he? GOD, how COULD he? How could he have come up to me and done that dreadful thing and then left me so heartlessly? God, I mean, I know it was only a parking ticket/no more than I deserved/his right as a pet hamster/the third ancient law of Emvu2tlnvdop'dn. But HOW COULD HE???? Again, less is more.

Rewrite any sentence that you have to read twice. You'll be amazed how readily this will happen once you've had at least a month away from your own work.

Systematically go through and check first and last lines. That means first and last lines of chapters AND first and last lines of scenes i.e. the lines either side of any line space. I just did this with a book of mine and discovered that in the space of about forty pages I had ended three times with 'as I was about to discover…'

After you macro-edit and before you micro-edit, approach the job armed with a list of opportunities for foreshadowing that you might previously have missed. Be alert, then, to places where you can slip in these key things.

General

Make sure you've written that synopsis of your novel before attempting any sort of edit. (See? That's why I put editing *after* the bit on writing synopses.) In distilling your great work into a page or two of summary (I'd attempt both) you will more clearly see what the book is trying to achieve. Once you've done that you will have a clearer sense of its theme, the nature of your protagonist's journey, and the structure of the plot.

Finally, know when to stop and let the experts decide. And if you do solicit outside input at this stage be clear, before soliciting it, what you hope to gain from it. I can't emphasis the importance of going through this thought process enough. If someone tells you, 'the second half of this book just didn't work for me' what are you going to do with that information?

A) get another opinion?
B) re-write it?
C) ignore it if you don't agree with it/didn't expect it?

Be very clear, because once that genie is out of the bottle emotionally, you can't get it back in.

Consider this:

If you decide A) you've already proved that you aren't 100% sure of this person's credentials for critiquing your book. In which case, seek more than one opinion in the first place. And be clear, when you do, what your next strategy will be. If they both say the same, are you going to trust them *now*? What if they completely disagree? Be honest with yourself with this. Or seek none, and trust your own judgement.

If you think you'd plump for B) then you obviously DO trust your reader. In which case, feel free to amend as they suggest. Do remember, however, that it's really easy to recognise that a novel isn't working. And is great deal harder, as a reader, to be able to explain why. Harder still to suggest how to fix it once it's written. (See 'stonking great outline' on page one.)

If C) is your choice, then you are soliciting advice for confidence purposes; reassurance that it's as good as you think it is – which means you don't really want to be told that it's not. If it will upset you for that to happen, then just don't go there. Be your own best editor. Go it alone.

A short homily on layout

And yes, I do mean homily. Not this the religious sense, though, by God, I feel strongly enough about it, but in the sense of it being a 'tedious moralising lecture', which is right up my street in this regard.

If you are a genius (and everyone can see you are a genius just by looking at half a dozen of your perfectly chosen words) then, of course, you can submit work in any way you like. But for most of us, our lights partly obscured beneath various bushels, there is no reason to ignore the conventions of written fiction (as published in the English language) when submitting our work.

Post the internet, this is a shifting bank of dunes, and one that's still in motion, and since anyone can slap a book up on Kindle now (and many do) there are some fine examples of just how loud is the still small voice of ignorance when it comes to making written work 'fit for market' before doing so. But in the world of professional publishing, being professional still matters, and if you want to be seen as a professional (which you absolutely do) then it's worth taking the trouble to lay out your work in what's a pretty universal publishing industry standard. Which is:

YOUR TITLE – like everything, in minimum 12 point
By
Your Name Here – using an unfussy font

The first thing to note when you are writing almost any form of fiction, is that there's a definite convention for layout. As you can see from the line above, the first line of your story is NOT* indented.

Second and subsequent paragraphs, however, always are. This holds true for dialogue, as well.

'Does it?' asked Julia, when we discussed it last week.

'Yes, it does,' I said. 'You should also note that whenever a new person speaks, you indent – treat it as a new paragraph.' I paused then, to let this bit of wisdom sink in. 'But when the same person speaks again,' I pointed out, 'you don't indent. Got that?'

'Got that,' she said.

Fast forward, as one does, to some point in the future, upon which, when writing fiction, we can use a device called a line break, as I've just done. I wasn't sure Julia would grasp that (what with Julia being Julia) but I remained confident that she would get the hang of it in the end.

'Anything else to add?' she wanted to know, over coffee. So I filled her in on all the important little details, such as double-spacing your work so it's easier on the eye (and leaves room for comments) and leaving spaces after punctuation such as full stops and commas. I also pointed out that TV programmes and songs (*EastEnders*, *White Christmas*) should always be rendered in italics, that the use of numbers and acronyms were issues of house-style (i.e. your individual publisher will deal with it), and that a single speech mark – 'like this' – was the norm for most organs (particularly in the UK), but that there was really no substitute for checking.

Finally, I drew her attention to the footer, which is located at the bottom of the page – every page – and should be pretty self-explanatory. Include the page number, the title and your name. Oh, and don't forget the word count. Which you should include at...

THE END

*if you are reading this on an e-reader you'll probably have noticed that I don't seem to be taking my own advice here. Conventions for Kindle and other devices are changing so quickly that I stuggle to keep up. That said, the print market still largely conforms to the same layout conventions it has for several decades. If in doubt, pick up a paperback novel, and you'll be in doubt no longer. I'd still submit using that convention, every time.

Step 12 – Selling it

It's an interesting but little understood truth that the word 'reader' can have many meanings, and unless you opt for going it alone and self-publishing, almost all of them are going to impact on your novel's progress, before it finally ends up in a 'proper' reader's hands. What follows is taken from a piece that appeared in a journal called The Bookseller, written by Horace Bent:

'Readers,' he explains, 'for the purposes of flogging a book, can be defined thus:

Agent: reading an MS implies eye contact with the name of the author printed on the top sheet, and the sensation of a six figure sum as a result of the subsequent cognitive process

Editorial director: a manuscript is considered read if it has not been lost on the way back to the office from lunch

Copy editor: has a unique ability to read only the words that should not be there

Bookseller: reading a book involves looking at the blurb and the jacket

Large chain bookseller: reading a book involves looking at the jacket

Occasionally, when they are on holiday, book-trade people discover the ordinary meaning of the verb 'to read'. They return to their offices as raving neophytes to a new age cult. Usually they can be calmed by a reminder that they had already 'read' the object of their enthusiasm and declared it to be an unpublishable dog.'

Horace makes a very important point here. In short, that the actual content of your novel will go from being supremely important to not-at-all important the further you get along the production process. Criminal though it seems, the people responsible for deciding whether to stock your book in their shop *will not have read it*. This is because – and this *is* logical – your book is being published for one reason only, that it was already considered brilliant enough (amid all those thousands of competitors) to have been chosen for publication in the first place. After that, it's all about the packaging.

I should mention, at this point, that there are other routes to publication, for which the terrible odds for getting to this heady place are a great deal shorter. They are called ' being a celebrity' and, er…. 'being a celebrity', where 'being a celebrity' is defined, very loosely, as being anyone whose fame or notoriety, *for whatever reason*, will ensure public interest, column inches, and big sales. This category includes reality stars, actors/musicians/TV presenters/sports people who also 'have a book in them', heroes of any description, villains, badly abused children Who Have Prevailed, relatives of high profile celebrities/politicians/publishers, authors who live next door to previously bestselling writers who now have Alzheimer's (the 'with A Famous Writer' phenomenon) and animals.

You are not them. So your book has to be better than almost anything any of them are likely to produce. But do not be downhearted. You will probably have a subsequent career. They probably won't. If they do, it'll be because they deserve it.

So what's an agent, and why do I need one?

A literary agent is a person whose business is to look after a 'stable' of authors; finding publishers for their books, negotiating terms on their behalf, together with the myriad tasks that are related to both functions including (one hopes) holding their hands – at least metaphorically, and in some cases, actually.

There are a few key things you should know about their function:

An agent is on *your* side. This sometimes needs emphasising. Yes, they usually have cordial and ongoing relationships with publishers and it can sometimes seem as if they are all part of some big exclusive lunching club, to which you've not been extended an invite. But that's not true. An agent is on your side because it's you they represent. Their income derives from your own publishing income – you pay them, so they want you to do well.

Literary agents' commission is usually between 10 and 15 percent of your income, where 'income' means money you make from your books – from advances, from royalties, from the sale of subsidiary rights (translation, serial, audio book and so on) as well as film and TV rights.

Terms vary according to agent, of course, but many will take 10% for home income and 20% for foreign deals (since this will be shared with a foreign sub-agent), others 15% across the board.

An agent who is a member of the Association of Authors' Agents (www.agentsassoc.co.uk) is part of a self-regulatory body and adheres to a professional code of practice. Which is not to say agents who aren't are no good (you have to have been in business for a minimum of 3 years to become a member, so a new kid on the block can't join yet, even if they're going to be brilliant) but if they are, you know what to expect.

Almost all good literary agents will read your work for free. If they charge a reading fee, my instinct would be to move on to the next one. One of the mantras I learned early and have never had cause to doubt is that, unless you are self-publishing, **at no point in the process** (unless you feel compelled to employ the services of, say, a professional proof reader, mentor or editor) **should you pay anyone for doing anything related to the publication of your book** (see below). The money – when it does flow – should be flowing *your* way.

A literary agent will almost always earn you way more money than you pay them in commission. This is an important thing to know. It's easy to persuade yourself you can go it alone but, quite apart from the fact that an agent is your primary route to an editor (only route, in many cases) they know publishing contracts like the backs of their hands and will ensure you get a better deal than you probably could alone. They also spare you the grubby and potentially antagonistic business of talking money with your publisher.

Literary agents, as a group, do not hate you. Nor do they spend their days gleefully pinging off curt 'thanks but no thanks' emails. They want nothing more than to discover the next J K Rowling, or Lee Child, or David Walliams, or Dan Brown. They open your attachment with the same thrill of anticipation that you experienced when attaching it to your email and pressing 'send'. They want you published. And published big. That's their dream.

Sadly, this happens rather less often than they'd like because, just as night follows day, much of what they get, in both inbox and post, is – sorry to be blunt about this – terrible.

Happily (and you must believe this or you should not be entering the fray here) *your* novel is a gem waiting to be discovered. So, without further wittering, we move on to the important bit – the basics of agent-getting best practice....

Getting a Literary Agent – another tick list

One of the things that I can guarantee one of my novel writing students (often several) will say to me at the start of every new term is 'what I really want to know is how to get an agent.' They invariably add – slightly hastily – that they also wish 'to find out how best to write a novel, *obviously*,' but there's no doubt a few students come to me having already written several novels and who turn up not only to learn aspects of the craft but also in the hopes of getting those vital contacts. I know a fair few agents. This, to the unpublished, is often key. So how exactly *do* you bag yourself one?

First of all, let's be clear on one fact. You are about to enter into a highly competitive industry. Remember that old statistic – that at any given time 75% of professional actors are out of work? Well, keep that n mind as you read. It's the reason most parents, when their wide-eyed child says 'I want to be an actor' throw their hands up in horror and then, over a sustained period of stealthy effort, redirect their ambitions into, say, insurance, or retail management. It's the same reason why, I now realise, and when I told my careers teacher at school that I 'wanted to be an author' she gave me a clutch of pamphlets about how to join the WRENS.

So that's clear, yes? You're up against it. There's no doubt about it. Many perfectly readable books remain in the wilderness for their authors' lifetimes; never published, never feted, never read. And no, it's not fair. It's pretty harsh. But it's also fact. The sort of fact that is best chewed over at length, duly digested and then, like that execrable fish bouillon you had in La Rochelle in 1976, altogether best expunged from your conscious mind.

To be replaced by wall-to-wall positivity and a 'sleeves up and get on with it' approach. With this attitude, you can quickly get ahead of the game. There have been many words written (particularly, now, on the internet) about the proper way to maximise your chances of being successful in this, the most elusive of all the writing stages (arguably), all of which are available to anyone who takes the time and trouble to look them up and actually *read* them. Happily, for you, lots of people don't think to do this, which reduces the competition at a stroke.

Nor do they avail themselves of the key resource in this respect, which is:

The Writers' and Artists' Yearbook

If you type 'UK literary agent' into a search engine, you will find yourself with an *embarras du richesses* of them to wade through. Far easier is to either buy The Writers' and Artists' Yearbook (around £15) or visit their website: https://www.writersandartists.co.uk. Here, for a subscription of £25, you will be able to access up-to-date listings for pretty much all reputable literary agents, *and what they are looking for*, as well as a host of other useful info. It really is the gold standard of directories.

Remember to make a note of that financial outlay, by the way. Not to mention others, such as printer ink, that new laptop, research trips to Venice etc., etc., as, once you are paid for your work, they will become tax-deductible.

Also remember to take the business of identifying potential agents seriously. It may feel like an 'any port in a storm' situation right now (they hold all the cards, because you hold all the desperate hope) but, if you are successful, this will be the beginning of a professional relationship that could endure for many years, and, hopefully, a mutually loyal friendship. And if you are lucky enough to attract the attention of more than one, take your time considering not just how well-connected/dynamic/busy with already successful authors they seem to be, but also whether you get along with them. You really do need to like and respect them. It's far more crucial than for editors, who tend to come and go, and dance to the publisher's tune, not yours. (Though I've worked with some wonderful editors, too.)

So take your time, read agents' blogs and biographies, compile a shortlist. Do sufficient homework that by the time you are ready to make submissions you have winnowed your list down to a handful of people you have a fighting chance of interesting in your work.

Assuming you've done, or are going to do this, and because all agents require slightly different things from submissions, there's no need for me to tell you what they are, except in the briefest of terms. Which are that:

Your submission should, almost always, include the following:

A short email – do not ramble or include unnecessary/irrelevant details; just say who you are, whether you have had previous work published (and, if so, what and where), a few lines about your book – that whole 'theme in two sentences' thing we discussed at the outset – and, if applicable, any small thing that you feel might enhance its chance of publication/success. (This is where those pesky celebs have the edge.)

Your submission, including:

A cover page, detailing the title and word count, with your contact details neatly in the corner.

The first three chapters or so of your novel, with professional layout and punctuation, double-spaced, and in a font large enough to be easily read. *Always* the first three – why would anyone NOT do that? This is storytelling, not a manual on how to keep fish.

A synopsis. Again, agents vary re length, but most follow the 'less is more' rule. Your synopsis, as we've already discussed, will be a work of art in itself. If your three chapters grab the agent, then look upon your synopsis as the only thing standing between you and a potentially life-changing phone call saying 'loved it, can I please see the rest?'.

And that's it. That's your basic submission package.

Other things you might consider

Using the phone. If you are confident and articulate, don't be afraid to call an agent, introduce yourself and actually *ask* them if they think they might be interested in you submitting your three chapters-and-synopsis. If the conversation goes well, and they like the sound of your proposal, they will remember your name when it comes in.

Networking. If you get the chance (having friends who are also more experienced writers are good for this) get yourself invited along to any place agents might be found; Society of Authors events, Romantic novelists Association events, writer's conferences, workshops, day schools etc. Be ready to ingratiate yourself and always keep business/contact cards with you (lots of online printers do them for next to nothing). Don't be afraid to ask them if they'd look at your novel. Remember what I've already said – talented new clients are most agents' and publishers' lifeblood, and, like you, they are always dreaming of bestsellerdom.

Gimmicks. My dear friend Jane Wenham-Jones snagged the interest – if not, sadly, on that occasion, the signature on the dotted line – of an agent (a premier league one, to boot) after seeing a piece in a paper in which he'd written that he just hated authors who sent him mss in ridiculously teeny tiny fonts. So she faxed him an enquiry (this was back in the late 1990s)

I hope this typeface is big enough for you

He was so amused that he faxed back that she could send the whole ms by first class post, and had read it by the end of that week.

Clearly this sort of approach won't work for everyone – those not involved in rom coms (this was really covert flirting, of course – don't rule it out) might need other sorts of gimmicks. They don't work with everyone, and some actively dislike them, but if you feel it might be worth a shot, then feel free to use your imagination. You're a novel writer, after all, so you have one.

Other things you might consider

Chances of winning the lottery: slim

Chances of being picked up from the slush pile of a major publisher; slimmer

Chances of being picked up by a major publisher through a good agent who believe in you and your talent: reasonably good

There is no getting around the fact that almost all authors need agents. Aside from the obvious reasons (they will fight your corner, negotiate better terms and sell other kinds of rights in your work, as already discussed) you need to accept that big publishers hardly ever find their new authors without them. I'll say that again – **big publishers hardly ever find their new authors without them.**

It stands to reason, therefore, that having one will increase your odds of being published by something like an order of magnitude. Yes, you might have heard the mantra 'it's harder to get an agent than a publisher' but this is only true if the publisher is a small press, for whom agents are often not a part of the process. This is often because they are generally offered work by authors who first tried, but then couldn't get an agent. Which is logical; if I were an agent trying to earn a living of 15%, I would try to place my clients' books with big publishers. (Big publishers generally mean vastly bigger sales.)

By all means, explore every possible alternative avenue to publication (see below) but remember, there is no magic bullet. Even with the massive explosion in book publishing (and, per capita, the UK is still the number one publisher of books in the world, closely followed by North America) there are still vastly more manuscripts out there than publishing slots – perhaps because, these days, with desktop publishing, ebooks, and a general reduction in physical effort involved in writing books, everyone is at it. Time was when anyone not born into wealth (or, indeed, a male) would not have a cat in hell's chance of getting published. No more.

So, yes, it's hard. All you can do is shorten the odds. A part of which will mean observing sensible rules of engagement, and another part – a big one – will mean embarking on another novel even while you're engaged in combat. You are a writer, so please don't stop writing at this point – remember, when your novel *does* sell, the publisher will want another, and quick. At all times think like a pavement artist: If this gets washed away, I can always do another.

Things agents hate (yup, another tick list)

Writers mentioning that their sister/lover/the woman down the road who was once published in a parish magazine loved it.

Pages of irrelevant CV – only mention that you shared a cell with Jeffery Archer for two years if it's relevant to the story or its chances of getting sold. Actually, if you shared a cell with Jeffery Archer for two years, mention it – **IN BOLD.** Just don't mention your swimming certificates.

Fancy typefaces and coloured fonts.

Cover mock ups. Oh, purlease! How arrogant!

Writers describing their own work as funny. That's not an assumption they are entitled to make.

Writers describing their own work as funny, and then adding 'my mum laughed like a drain'.

Writers sending non-sequential chapters on the grounds that they are 'the best bits' – the ones they'll get to after they have waded through the dreary beginning. I hope it's clear to you how flawed this thinking is, I really do. Quite apart from the fact that reading chapter 17 in isolation will render it largely meaningless, *every* bit of your book must be a best bit.

Writers saying they have written the whole novel and then not quite having done so.

Writers writing 'I know it says in the Writer's Handbook that you don't accept Sci Fi, but I thought it would be a profitable addition to your list'.

Writers very obviously sending multiple submissions (also see below). Obviously few are dim enough to address their enquiry letter 'dear agent', but a little effort, as in 'I saw that you represent… insert name of fabulously successful author on that particular agent's list…' makes all the difference.

A note on Multiple Submissions

Attitudes have changed since I started back in the late 90s. At that time, you sent material to more than one agent simultaneously at your peril. This was not as unreasonable as it might first sound. After all, a reputable agent will not charge you a reading fee – they will read your work on the basis that it might be good enough to make them rich. However, this means wading through a great deal of work that manifestly won't, so time is at a premium.

Nowadays, however, agents have come to realise that if a writers sends work to agents one at a time, and each agent then spends 3 months responding, the writer could potentially expire long before getting g published, and will most definitely die a little bit inside. It's generally accepted that writers will usually send three-chapters-and-a-synopsis to several agents at once. At this point, there's no need to provide these agents with details of each other.

If an agent comes back to you and asks for the rest of the ms they will often, at this point, ask if it's out elsewhere. Now you must be honest. If they are the first to ask for the rest, you can obviously say 'no' (we're talking the whole ms now). If it already is (and well done you, by the way!), then you should really be upfront and admit it. Don't worry that this will put the agent off –quite the contrary; hopefully it will only increase their enthusiasm, by proving their instinct might be right. If they still want to see it themselves, then do send it – but remember that if you told the first agent they were reading it exclusively, then you really must come clean if you decide to branch out.

Obviously, if either agent asks no questions, then – woo hoo! – you can send it wherever you like. Just don't expect that to be the norm, though.

A word on rejection

Or, rather, three of them; *deal with it*. Also, try to understand that the pain of rejection when you are unpublished is simply your apprenticeship into a world in which, unless you are spectacularly lucky, will continue to be an everyday part of your working life. That sounds harsh, I know, but it's true. Having a single novel published does not a career make. Yes, a few writers do start writing, get published and continue to get published, their careers growing in eminence and lustre as they go. But that's not the norm. Like many a career in the creative and artistic firmament, your star will brighten and perhaps fade, before shining again in a different galaxy, or – again, I know it's brutal – it might just disappear into a black hole. Just as it with pop stars, today's next big thing can all too soon become yesterday's has been.

But don't be downhearted. If you are a writer than, like me, you probably can't not write, and once you are published – in any small way – you have a weapon in your armoury that you didn't previously have; whatever the erratic nature of your fortunes along the way, no-one can take your back catalogue away from you, which will encourage you in the business of creating more. You have already crossed a line that so many never will – so you have proof that your faith in yourself was not misplaced.

This comforting fact will go further than you think during dark times and lean times, to keep a flame of self-belief alight in your breast. You must, however, learn to make sensible distinctions – between the sort of rejection that is a reflection on your work (in which case, grab all the advice you can and if it strikes a chord, act upon it) and the sort of rejection that is nothing to do with you i.e. simply a manifestation of an overcrowded market, a clash of interest with someone on an agent's current list, the demand for what you're doing being temporarily sated, a novel in your genre having just been placed with a particular publisher, or the agent having a hated aunt with the same name as you. And yes – this does sometimes happen…

To self-publish or no…

The evolution of self-publishing in the last ten years or so has been an incredibly swift one. I've followed its fortunes as both an observer and a participant, as, a few years ago, I regained the rights to a few of my early rom-coms and re-issued them myself. In the early days, this was astonishingly lucrative, as Amazon set up systems which gave self-published authors the opportunity to promote their books by offering them for free (we are talking ebook versions here) for a short period – usually five days – which put them quickly at the top of their charts. This meant no revenue, of course, but it brought the book to the attention of readers who might then pay for another of your titles and also, via whatever algorithmic alchemy they were them using, created a tail of visibility when they reverted to having a cost attached, which, in some cases, produced a decent wodge of actual money, before they were once again submerged into the general book swamp.

Two things then happened. Amazon, whether driven by reader behaviour or otherwise, created a two channel system for books. There were readers who bought books (from any publisher) and paid for them, as per usual, and others, whose choices were dictated by cost. Some would only buy books on promotion for 99p, and others would only 'buy' free ones. I remember having a review once that included 'I'm glad I didn't pay for it'. (Remember, there are people who will happily pay £3.50 for a coffee, but see paying for a novel as a mug's game. A couple even exist in my middle class, mostly highly solvent, book club, keen to borrow someone else's dog-eared library copy rather than spend £6.99, with no thought about how authors make a living…)

The other development was an almost exponential growth in self-published authors, excited by all the stories of the self-published making fortunes, due to not having to share with pesky agents and publishers and wholesalers and retailers. (A typical royalty on a paperback – sobering, this – is 7.5% of the wholesale price.) It's true that a few made a great deal of money. Though most didn't, and for most, that ship has long sailed. I can't quote the actual dates and figures, but I recall reading that in a period of a couple of years, the number of self-published titles on Amazon rose from around 600,000 to around 4 million, so you can see the problem.

Today, incidentally, there is a large group of readers who still specialise in reading freebies, gathered loosely under the umbrella of being book-bloggers. They read ARCs, or Advance Reader Copies, in advance, as the name implies, of publication. Almost all the major publishers use them (my various publishers included), and they form a big part of any marketing push, as these readers then review the books (that's the contract – free book, for review purposes) and share their reviews with their followers, and, if the reviews are good, they generate both reviews and advance sales – two vital components of modern book-selling.

Not anyone can do it, however. Potential ARC readers go on the NetGalley site on a regular basis and choose books they fancy, and the publisher decides whether to give them one. As you'd expect, it comes down to how many followers/regular site visitors they have – a reviewer with tens of thousands of followers can 'spread' a book much like a virus.

If you choose to self-publish – and you might still want to, for all sorts of reasons – it pays to make yourself aware of how the market works, and to factor in one important thing. That, if you do, you will have to spend a LOT of time doing all the things publishers and agents do. Which will leave little time for actually writing.

So my message on self-publishing is twofold. First, please get your work professionally edited – don't skip this. If you love language, please, please don't litter the Internet with shoddy, grammatically offensive work. My second message is simple too – it's an unequivocal 'please proceed with caution'.

Think:

how much time you want to spend selling books rather than writing them (and trust me the US tax forms are a nightmare.....), because just as in the olden days the self-published author had to traipse the streets trying to sell half a dozen physical books to independent bookshops (chains won't entertain them), so today's ebook self-publisher has to REALLY like doing business; getting your stuff out there can easily become a full time job. And one with decidedly unreliable results.

whether you're confident it will make you happy. If the idea of running your own thriving ebook cottage industry floats your boat, then go ahead – why ever wouldn't you? And who knows? If you hit the spot with enough readers then you *will* get that validation, and can tell all the agents and publishers who dissed you to go and take a running jump. But, again, do stop and think, because I've spoken to several who've done it and they've received scant sales, scant validation and without question, scant happiness, seeing such success as they've had as a poor second best. It's perhaps that old truism – they still want to see their name, on a book, in a bookshop, with the name of a respected and successful publishing imprint on the spine. And, at the time of writing, self-publishing ebooks just doesn't deliver that kick.

If you can see it as a means to an end. Get your manuscript professionally edited (again, please, oh please, pay to do that) get it up there and give it a limited amount of your attention, while concentrating the greater part of your emotional and physical energies to pursuing traditional publication and – crucially – to getting on with your next.

It's impossible for me to know what I'd be doing if I was starting out now but I'm inclined to think, if I didn't get an agent pretty quickly, that, impatient for action, I would give serious thought to dabbling in ebook self-publishing, but definitely, *only*, in the spirit of **c)**. My main focus would still be the same as it ever was. Write the next, write the next, write the next.

Vanity/Hybrid publishers – a third way?

So called 'Vanity' publishers mostly do what they say on the tin – pander to an author's vanity, at a price. It sounds harsh (no one wants to consider themselves vain), but such publishers have existed, and presumably profitably, for decades. This is because there are sufficient authors out there who, mostly having failed to attract and agent or traditional publisher, are willing to pay someone to publish and market their book. 'Never go to a vanity publisher' is probably one of the earliest pieces of writing advice I can remember getting.

The reasons, as were explained to me, were twofold. 1, that they would probably tell you your book was better than it was (logical, if their objective was to part someone from their money) and 2, that, having already got your money, they had little incentive to market the resulting work, preferring to rely on the author to do that job themselves, not least by going on to buy lots of copies to distribute among friends and family. All of which is a logical business model. It also reinforces the point that a publisher who has paid YOU for your book has the motivation to be sure it is the best book it can be, and to market it well, so that their investment in you pays.

Hybrid publishers are a modern tweak on the above. The same basic rules apply (your book will gather more plaudits than it perhaps deserves, and you will have to part with money) but they are slightly different in that they tend to talk in terms of 'sharing' the production costs; providing a suite of services that seem genuinely to have the ambition to make the book successful.

I've had no personal dealings with either kind of publisher, but will say this. The internet is a mine of information about both the model and about specific players in this field. So, before parting with any money, think about *why* someone might be telling you your book is suddenly the best thing since sliced bread, and practice due diligence in researching the company.

My opinion? (There are others.) After years in the business, I still think the traditional model works. Though gems do get missed, the agent/professional publisher model remains the best. It acts as a valuable filter, and delivers what the majority of readers expect – something well-put together and scrupulously edited, while leaving authors to do what they do best; provide the talent and raw materials. So I'd always counsel going down the agent road as a first step. And if you have no luck in attracting wither an agent or a traditional publisher, I'd seriously consider self-publishing as the best alternative. It gives you total control of both the book and the process and, if you put your heart and soul into it, and make it sufficiently visible, there is always the chance that a traditional publisher will spot it and offer you a multi-book publishing deal.

Finally

With the best will in the world, no one can predict how long it will take you to achieve publication. For some it happens quickly, for others very slowly – some authors have written many, many novels before they sell one (famously, Joanne Harris, author of *Chocolat*, springs to mind), while others enjoy overnight success.

In some cases this is because what they've written is so universal and/or groundbreaking and/or brilliant that it strikes a chord with everyone who reads it, while with others, it's simply perfect timing, for a competent, fresh voice – but one that could, even so, be one of many with equal claim. Don't let this depress you. Remember – ordinary readers will always need 'ordinary' books i.e. ones that slot perfectly into a genre that they enjoy.

You can do nothing about this situation, either way. All you can do is either keep going or give up, and importantly, if you decide to choose the first path, keep shortening the odds by getting your work out there. And if you do end up in a position where you've exhausted all the possibilities in the *Writers' and Artists' Yearbook*, then, if you've followed my advice and kept writing, you'll by this time have a brand new novel with which to wow them, and this one – I guarantee it – will be even better than the first.

Good luck!

About the Author

Born in London, I began my writing career as a teenager, when I was 'discovered' by a London-based literary agent, Annie Hallam, via a fan letter I sent to an actor who was her friend. Though life and love took precedence and I didn't actually achieve publication then, I returned to my first love in 1994, as a mother of three, newly transplanted to Cardiff. My first paid-for piece of writing was a short article about being a mature primary school teacher training student, published in the Times Education Supplement. It's fair to say my world changed that day. Rather than apply for a teaching post (as would have been sensible), I instead applied myself, cutting my teeth writing short stories for the then still lucrative world of women's lifestyle magazines.

I have been a fulltime author since the mid 1990s. These days, I mostly spend my time writing psychological thrillers (including *Can You See Me?* and *False Hope*, both under the pseudonym Lynne Lee) but I'm also the author of eight romantic comedies, and one random outlier, in the shape of *Able Seacat Simon*; a novel based on the true story of – and narrated by – a famous naval cat.

I diversified into ghostwriting in 2007 and have since ghosted 26 full-length non-fiction memoirs, most of which have been UK Sunday Times bestsellers. My titles include *Giant George; life with the world's biggest dog*, and *The Girl With No Name; the incredible true story of a girl raised by monkeys*, which has now been published in 27 countries.

I don't just work with animals. Other publications include *On Duty For The Queen*, for former UK Royal Press Secretary Dickie Arbiter, and the heartbreaking story of the Rebecca Aylward murder, *Bye Mam, I Love You*, which has garnered over 700 five star reviews. I also co-wrote of the Julie Shaw series of gritty Bradford-based crime memoirs, the first of which, *Our Vinnie*, went straight into the bestseller lists, and am the incognito co-writer of a successful series of fostering memoirs, the eighteenth of which was published in August 2020.

But I do love working with animals. My most recent ghosted work (and probably my personal favourite) is <u>*Fabulous Finn*</u>, the story of a now famous police dog, who was stabbed, almost fatally, when on duty with his handler Dave Wardell. Now retired, Finn has gone on to win multiple prestigious awards for his bravery (including a PDSA Gold Medal) and is the face – I'd say icon – behind "Finn's Law"; new legislation to better protect our service animals.

Though I have yet to work as a primary school teacher, I've never lost the bug, and have been teaching novel writing and short story writing at Cardiff University's Continuing and Professional Education Department since 2009. My students (several of whom are now published authors) come from all backgrounds and have wildly different ambitions, but almost all share the same compulsion: to write. This manual is a distillation of my course, *Novel Writing Workshop*, including all the bits time constraints invariably mean get left out, an extended section on getting published and on the self-publishing revolution.

For more information about me and my work, please visit www.lynnebarrett-lee.com

www.ingramcontent.com/pod-product-compliance
Lightning Source LLC
Chambersburg PA
CBHW021933040426
42448CB00008B/1046